FLOWER FABLES

FLOWER FABLES

BY

LOUISA MAY ALCOTT

"Pondering shadows, colors, clouds,
Grass-buds, and caterpillar shrouds,
Boughs on which the wild bees settle,
Tints that spot the violet's petal."
—EMERSON'S WOOD-NOTES.

WITH 34 ILLUSTRATIONS.

Published in Cooperation with
Louisa May Alcott's Orchard House
Concord, Massachusetts

APPLEWOOD BOOKS
Bedford, Massachusetts

Flower Fables was first published in 1854. The pages in this edition are reproduced from the Henry Altemus edition published in Philadelphia in 1898.

For more information about Louisa May Alcott's Orchard House visit www.louisamayalcott.org.

Thank you for purchasing an Applewood Book.
Applewood reprints America's lively classics—books from the past that are still of interest to modern readers.
For a free copy of our current catalog, write to:
Applewood Books, P.O. Box 365, Bedford, MA 01730

ISBN 978-1-55709-954-9

10 9 8 7 6 5 4 3

INTRODUCTION

"Fairyland" was familiar territory to young Louisa May Alcott and her sisters, for they had often romped there and explored its secrets under the guidance of family friend Henry David Thoreau. Fifteen years her elder, Thoreau led the Alcott girls and their friends on berry-picking expeditions in the wooded land around Walden Pond, which he fancifully called "Fairyland." It was on a piece of this land, owned by neighbor Ralph Waldo Emerson, that the girls' father, Amos Bronson Alcott, helped Thoreau build the now-famous cabin where he lived "deliberately" and wrote *Walden*.

> *I went to the woods because I wished to live deliberately, to front only the essential facts of life, and see if I could not learn what it had to teach, and not, when I came to die, discover that I had not lived.* (WALDEN, CH. 2)

The remarkable convergence of 19th century writers in Concord, Massachusetts may be glimpsed in this collection of stories inspired during visits to Walden Woods. The Alcott family often visited Thoreau to swim in the cove near his cabin or explore the changing seasons in this tranquil spot.

> *I had three chairs in my house; one for solitude, two for friendship, three for society. When visitors came in larger and unexpected numbers there was but the third chair for them all, but they generally economized the room by standing up. It is surprising how many great men and women a small house will contain. I have had twenty-five or thirty souls, with their bodies, at once under my roof,*

*and yet we often parted without being aware that we had
come very near to one another.* (WALDEN, CH. 6)

With Thoreau as a guide, Louisa and the other children
learned much about nature, but Louisa in particular delighted in
another aspect of Thoreau's point of view. The very fact that he
called the woods "Fairyland" opened up a new way of thinking in
the young writer's mind. Whether he pointed out a new animal
track, made a perfect bird call, or discovered a bit of a cobweb and
called it a fairy's handkerchief, it was all magic to Louisa and fod-
der for her lively imagination.

On many of her walks around Walden, Louisa shared original
fairy stories with her sisters, Thoreau, and friends. One of these
young friends was Ellen, the daughter of Ralph Waldo Emerson.
Six years her junior, Ellen admired Louisa the way Louisa looked
up to Thoreau. Ellen was so captivated by the fairy stories that
Louisa eventually wrote them down as a present for her. The entire
Emerson family noticed and delighted in their young neighbor's
generous gift, and shared their pleasure with Louisa's father.

Mr. Alcott was equally impressed with his daughter's stories. He
was a complex and unusual man—a genius, according to Emerson.
He was a remarkable father, if an uncertain provider. He believed in
encouraging children—even girls—to follow their dreams.

The norm of the day was not to allow young ladies to tax
themselves with such "brain work" as writing. The rest of Boston
society might have considered writing an improper occupation for
a lady, but Mr. Alcott was proud and excited by his daughter's talent. He carried her fairy stories to George W. Briggs, a new pub-
lisher on Washington Street in Boston. Briggs decided to take a
chance and agreed to publish Louisa's fairy stories under the title
Flower Fables.

Advance copies came out in time for Louisa to give them as gifts for the Christmas of 1854. How thrilled Ellen Emerson must have been to read the dedication in her friend's first published book:

To
ELLEN EMERSON,
FOR WHOM THEY WERE FANCIED, THESE
FLOWER FABLES
ARE INSCRIBED, BY HER FRIEND,
THE AUTHOR

Boston, Dec. 9, 1854.

Louisa also provided Ellen with her own copy and this Christmas note:

Dear Ellen,

Hoping that age has not lessened your love for the *Fairy folk* I have ventured to place your name in my little book, for your interest in their sayings and doings, first called forth these "Flower Fables," most of which were fancied long ago in Concord woods and fields. The pictures are not what I hoped they would be and it is very evident that the designer is not as well acquainted with fairy forms and faces as you and I are, so we must each *imagine* to suit ourselves and I hope if the fairies tell me any more stories, they will let an Elfin artist *illustrate* them. So dear Ellen will you accept the accompanying book, with many wishes for a merry "Christmas, and a happy New Year," from your friend,

Louisa M. Alcott.

Louisa took special pride in giving her mother a copy of the book. Mrs. Alcott was called "Marmee" by her daughters as was Mrs. March in the highly autobiographical *Little Women*. She read the following inscription in her copy of *Flower Fables*:

20 Pinckney Street, Boston, Dec. 25, 1854.

Dear Mother,—Into your Christmas stocking I have put my "first born," knowing that you will accept it with all its faults (for grandmothers are always kind), and look upon it merely as an earnest of what I may yet do, for, with so much to cheer me on, I hope to pass in time from fairies and fables to men and realities.

Whatever beauty or poetry is to be found in my little book is owing to your interest in and encouragement of all my efforts from the first to the last, and if ever I do anything to be proud of, my greatest happiness will be that I can thank you for that, as I may do for all the good there is in me; and I shall be content to write if it gives you pleasure.

Jo is fussing about,
My lamp is going out.

To dear mother, with many kind wishes for a happy New Year and merry Christmas.

I am your ever loving daughter
Louy.

Long before Louisa wrote *Little Women* or her now public "blood and thunder" tales, the publication of these fairy stories confirmed the hopes of this fledgling author that she might, indeed, succeed. The woodland sprites and struggling human children who encounter them evoke those idyllic walks with Thoreau and the tom-boyish prototype of Jo March, "Louy Alcott," who struggled with her conscience every bit as much as her character "Annie" in "Little Annie's Dream: or The Fairy Flower."

> ". . . now, dear Annie," said the Fairy, bending nearer, "tell me why I found no sunshine on your face. . ."
> "Ah, you will not love me any more if I should tell you all," said Annie, while the tears began to fall again; "I am not happy, for I am not good; how shall I learn to be a patient, gentle child? Good little Fairy, will you teach me how?"

These stories provide a fresh look at a complex author. Due to the success of *Little Women* and subsequent children's books, Louisa was well known as "The Children's Friend." She was less known as "Nurse Tribulation Periwinkle" in *Hospital Sketches*, written after she served as a nurse for the Union Army during the Civil War. She was completely unknown in her own lifetime as "A. M. Barnard," a prolific author of provocative thrillers. Today, many readers delight in those thrillers, but know nothing of her first published book, *Flower Fables*.

Orchard House is proud to offer this commemorative edition of *Flower Fables* on the 150th anniversary of its publication. All proceeds from the sale of this edition will benefit the home where Louisa wrote and set *Little Women*, Orchard House in Concord, Massachusetts. Known as "Apple Slump" to Louisa and her mother, this 1690s farmhouse has come to require a great deal of tender—and costly—care in order to save it from collapse. Thanks to initial funding from *Save America's Treasures*, the first phase of its preservation is complete and includes a foundation where none existed before. There is much more to do in order to stabilize interior walls and preserve such artifacts as the drawings that the youngest Alcott sister placed on the walls. Many dedicated individuals are committed to continuing preservation work on the home until the "*Little Women* House," as it is often known, is secure for future generations of readers. Please log onto *www.louisamayalcott.org*, if you would like to support this effort.

Many visitors comment that they enjoy Orchard House because they feel as if they are "walking through the book." Their enjoyment increases when they discover the complexity, talent, bravery, integrity and love of the real family that inspired *Little Women*. We at Orchard House hope that *Flower Fables* will be part of that discovery for you.

Happy reading!

JAN TURNQUIST
Executive Director, Louisa May Alcott's Orchard House
Concord, Massachusetts
Christmas 2004

TO

ELLEN EMERSON,

FOR WHOM THEY WERE FANCIED, THESE

FLOWER FABLES

ARE INSCRIBED, BY HER FRIEND,

THE AUTHOR

Boston, Dec. 9, 1854.

CONTENTS.

Flower Fables.

HE summer moon shone brightly down upon the sleeping earth, while far away from mortal eyes danced the Fairy folk. Fire-flies hung in bright clusters on the dewy leaves, that waved in the cool night-wind; and the flowers stood gazing in very wonder at the little Elves who lay among the fern-leaves, swung in the vine-boughs, sailed on the lake in lily cups, or danced on the mossy ground, to the music of the harebells, who rung out their merriest peal in honor of the night.

Under the shade of the wild rose sat the Queen and her little Maids of Honor, beside the silvery mushroom where the feast was spread.

"Now, my friends," said she, "to wile away the time till the bright moon goes down, let us each tell a tale, or relate what we have done or learned this day. I will begin with you, Sunny Lock," added she, turning to a lovely little Elf, who lay among the fragrant leaves of a primrose.

With a gay smile, "Sunny Lock" began her story.

"As I was painting the bright petals of a blue bell, it told me this tale."

The Frost King; or the Power of Love.

THREE little fairies sat in the fields
eating their breakfast; each among
the leaves of her favorite flower,
Daisy, Primrose, and Violet, were
as happy as elves need be.

The morning wind gently
rocked them to and fro, and the sun shone warmly
down upon the dewy grass, where butterflies
spread their gay wings, and bees with their deep
voices sung among the flowers; while the little
birds hopped merrily about to peep at them. On
a silvery mushroom was spread the breakfast;
little cakes of flower-dust lay on a broad green
leaf, beside a crimson strawberry, which, with

sugar from the violet, and cream from the yellow milkweed, made a fairy meal ; and their drink was the dew from the flowers' bright leaves.

"Ah me," sighed Primrose, throwing herself languidly back, "how warm the sun grows ! give me another piece of strawberry, and then I must hasten away to the shadow of the ferns. But while I eat tell me, dear Violet, why are you all so sad? I have scarce seen a happy face since my return from Rose Land ; dear friend, what means it?"

"I will tell you," replied little Violet, the tears gathering in her soft eyes. "Our good Queen is ever striving to keep the dear flowers from the power of the cruel Frost King ; many ways she tried, but all have failed. She has sent messengers to his court with costly gifts, but all have returned sick for want of sunlight, weary and sad ; we have watched over them, heedless of sun or shower, but still his dark spirits do their work, and we are left to weep over our blighted blossoms. Thus have we striven, and in vain, and this night our Queen holds council for the last time. Therefore are we sad, Primrose, for she

WATER VIOLETS.

has toiled and cared for us, and we can do nothing to help or advise her."

"It is indeed a cruel thing," replied her friend;
"but as we cannot help it, we must suffer patiently,
and not let the sorrows of others disturb our happiness. But, dear sisters, see you not how high
the sun is getting? I have my locks to curl, and
my robe to prepare for the evening; therefore I
must be gone, or I shall be brown as a withered
leaf in this warm light." So, gathering a tiny
mushroom for a parasol, she flew away; Daisy
soon followed, and Violet was left alone.

Then she spread the table afresh, and to it
came fearlessly the busy ant and bee, gay butterfly and bird; even the poor blind mole and
humble worm were not forgotten; and with gentle
words she gave to all, while each learned some-
thing of their kind teacher; and the love that
made her own heart bright shone alike on all.

The ant and the bee learned generosity, the
butterfly and the bird contentment, the mole and
worm confidence in the love of others, and each
went to their home better for the little time they
had been with the Violet.

Evening came, and with it troops of Elves to counsel their good Queen, who, seated on her mossy throne, looked anxiously upon the throng below, whose glittering wings and rustling robes gleamed like many-colored flowers.

At length she rose, and amid the deep silence spoke thus:

"Dear children, let us not tire of a good work, hard though it may be and wearisome; think of the many little hearts that in their sorrow look to us for help. What would the green earth be without its lovely flowers, and what a lonely home for us! Their beauty fills our hearts with brightness, and their love with tender thoughts. Ought we then to leave them to die uncared for and alone? They give to us their all; ought we not to toil unceasingly, that they may bloom in peace within their quiet homes? We have tried to gain the love of the stern Frost King, but in vain; his heart is hard as his own icy land; no love can melt, no kindness bring it back to sunlight and to joy. How then may we keep our frail blossoms from his cruel spirits? Who will give counsel? Who will be our messenger for the last time? Speak, my subjects."

Then a great murmuring arose, and many spoke, some for costlier gifts, some for war; and the fearful counselled patience and submission.

Long and eagerly they spoke, and their soft voices rose high.

The sweet music sounded on the air, and the loud tones were hushed, as in wondering silence the Fairies waited what should come.

Through the crowd there came a little form, a wreath of pure white violets lay among the bright locks that fell so softly round the gentle face, where a deep blush glowed, as, kneeling at the throne, little Violet said:

"Dear Queen, we have bent to the Frost-King's power, we have borne gifts unto his pride, but have we gone trustingly to him and spoken fearlessly of his evil deeds? Have we shed the soft light of unwearied love around his cold heart, and with patient tenderness shown him how bright and beautiful love can make the darkest lot?

"Our messengers have gone fearfully, and with cold looks and courtly words offered him rich gifts, things he cared not for, and with equal pride has he sent them back.

"Then let me, the weakest of your band, go to him, trusting in the love I know lies hidden in the coldest heart.

"I will bear only a garland of our fairest flowers; these will I wind about him, and their bright faces, looking lovingly in his, will bring sweet thoughts to his dark mind, and their soft breath steal in like gentle words. Then, when he sees them fading on his breast, will he not sigh that their is no warmth there to keep them fresh and lovely? This will I do, dear Queen, and never leave his dreary home, till the sunlight falls on flowers fair as those that bloom in our own dear land."

Silently the Queen had listened, but now, rising and placing her hand on little Violet's head, she said, turning to the throng below:

"We in our pride and power erred, while this, the weakest and lowliest of our subjects, has from the innocence of her own pure heart counselled us more wisely than the noblest of our train. All who will aid our brave little messenger, lift your wands, that we may know who will place their trust in the Power of Love."

Every fairy wand glistened in the air, as with silvery voices they cried, " Love, and little Violet."

Then down from the throne, hand in hand came the Queen and Violet, and till the moon sank did the fairies toil, to weave a wreath of the fairest flowers. Tenderly they gathered them, with the night-dew fresh upon their leaves, and as they wove chanted sweet spells, and whispered fairy blessings on the bright messengers whom they sent forth to die in a dreary land, that their gentle kindred might bloom unharmed.

At length it was done ; and the fair flowers lay glowing in the starlight, while beside them stood the fairies, singing to the music of the wind-harps :

E are sending
you, dear
flowers,
Forth alone to
die,
Where your gentle sisters may
not weep
O'er the cold graves where
you lie;
But you go to bring them
fadeless life
In the bright homes where
they dwell,
And you softly smile that 'tis so,
As we sadly sing farewell.

"O plead with gentle words
for us,
And whisper tenderly
Of generous love to that cold
heart,
And it will answer ye;

And though you fade in a dreary home,
    Yet loving hearts will tell
Of the joy and peace that you have given:
    Flowers, dear flowers, farewell!''

The morning sun looked softly down upon the broad green earth, which like a mighty altar was sending up clouds of perfume from its breath, while flowers danced gayly in the summer wind, and birds sang their morning hymn among the cool green leaves. Then high above, on shining wings, soared a little form. The sunlight rested softly on the silken hair, and the winds fanned lovingly the bright face, and brought the sweetest odors to cheer her on.

Thus went Violet through the clear air, and the earth looked smiling up to her, as, with the bright wreath folded in her arms, she flew among the soft, white clouds.

On and on she went, over hill and valley, broad rivers and rustling woods, till the warm sunlight passed away, the winds grew cold, and the air thick with falling snow. Then far below she saw the Frost-King's home. Pillars of hard,

BRAVE LITTLE VIOLET KNEELING AT THE FROST-KING'S THRONE.

gray ice supported the high, arched roof, hung with crystal icicles.   Dreary gardens lay around. filled with withered flowers and bare, drooping trees ; while heavy clouds hung low in the dark sky, and a cold wind murmured sadly through the wintry air.

With a beating heart Violet folded her fading wreath more closely to her breast, and with weary wings flew onward to the dreary palace.

Here, before the closed doors, stood many forms with dark faces and harsh voices, who sternly asked the shivering little fairy why she came to them.

Gently she answered, telling them her errand beseeching them to let her pass ere the cold wind blighted her frail blossoms ?   Then they flung wide the doors, and she passed in.

Walls of ice, carved with strange figures were around her ; glittering icicles hung from the high roof, and soft, white snow covered the hard floors. On a throne hung with clouds sat the Frost-King ; a crown of crystals bound his white locks, and a dark mantle wrought with delicate frost-work was folded over his cold breast.

His stern face could not stay little Violet, and on through the long hall she went, heedless of the snow that gathered at her feet, and the bleak wind that blew around her; while the King with wondering eyes looked on the golden light that played upon the dark walls as she passed.

The flowers, as if they knew their part, unfolded their bright leaves, and poured forth their sweetest perfume, as, kneeling at the throne, the brave little Fairy said,

"O King of blight and sorrow, send me not away till I have brought back the light and joy that will make your dark home bright and beautiful again. Let me call back to the desolate gardens the fair forms that are gone, and their soft voices blessing you will bring to your breast a never failing joy. Cast by your icy crown and sceptre, and let the sunlight of love fall softly on your heart.

"Then will the earth bloom again in all its beauty, and your dim eyes will rest only on fair forms, while music shall sound through these dreary halls, and the love of grateful hearts be yours. Have pity on the gentle flower-spirits,

Flower Fables—2

and do not doom them to an early death, when they might bloom in fadeless beauty, making us wiser by their gentle teachings, and the earth brighter by their lovely forms. These fair flowers, with the prayers of all Fairy Land, I lay before you; O send me not away till they are answered."

And with tears falling thick and fast upon their tender leaves, Violet laid the wreath at his feet, while the golden light grew ever brighter as it fell upon the little form so humbly kneeling there.

The King's stern face grew milder as he gazed on the gentle Fairy, and the flowers seem to look beseechingly upon him; while the fragrant voices sounded softly in his ear, telling of their dying sisters, and of the joy it gives to bring happiness to the weak and sorrowing. But he drew the dark mantle closer over his breast and answered coldly,

"I cannot grant your prayer, little Fairy; it is my will the flowers should die. Go back to your Queen, and tell her that I can not yield my power to please these foolish flowers?"

Then Violet hung the wreath above the throne.

and with weary feet went forth again, out into the cold, dark gardens, and still the golden shadows followed her, and wherever they fell, flowers bloomed and green leaves rustled.

Then came the Frost-Spirits, and beneath their cold wings the flowers died, while the Spirits bore Violet to a low, dark cell, saying as they left her, that their King was angry that she dared to stay when he had bid her go.

So all alone she sat, and sad thoughts of her happy home came back to her, and she wept bitterly. But soon came visions of the gentle flowers dying in their forest homes, and their voices ringing in her ear, imploring her to save them. Then she wept no longer, but patiently awaited what might come.

Soon the golden light gleamed faintly through the cell, and she heard little voices calling for help, and high up among the heavy cobwebs hung poor little flies struggling to free themselves, while their cruel enemies sat in their nets, watching their pain.

With her wand the Fairy broke the bands that held them, tenderly bound up their broken wings, and healed their wounds ; while they lay in the

warm light, and feebly hummed their thanks to
their kind deliverer.

Then she went to the ugly brown spiders, and
in gentle words told them, how in Fairy Land
their kindred spun all the elfin cloth, and in return the Fairies gave them food, and then how
happily they lived among the cool green leaves;
spinning garments for their neighbors. "And
you, too," said she, "shall spin for me, and I will
give you better food than helpless insects. You
shall live in peace, and spin your delicate threads
into a mantle for the stern King; and I will weave
golden threads amid the gray, that when folded
over his cold heart gentle thoughts may enter in
and make it their home.

And while she gayly sung, the little weavers
spun their silken threads, the flies on glittering
wings flew lovingly above her head, and over all
the golden light shone softly down.

When the Frost-Spirits told their King, he
greatly wondered, and often stole to look at the
sunny little room where friends and enemies
worked peacefully together. Still the light grew
brighter, and floated out into the cold air, where

it hung like bright clouds above the dreary gardens, whence all the Spirits' power could not drive it; and green leaves budded on the naked trees, and flowers bloomed; but the Spirits heaped snow upon them, and they bowed their heads and died.

At length the mantle was finished, and amid the gray threads shone golden ones, making it bright; and she sent it to the King, entreating him to wear it, for it would bring peace and love to dwell within his breast.

But he scornfully threw it aside, and bade his Spirits take her to a colder cell, deep in the earth; and there with harsh words they left her.

Still she sang gayly on, and the falling drops kept time so musically, that the King in his cold ice-halls wondered at the low, sweet sounds that came stealing up to him.

Thus Violet dwelt, and each day the golden light grew stronger, and from among the crevices of the rocky walls came troops of little velvet-coated moles, praying that they might listen to the sweet music, and lie in the warm light.

"We lead," said they, "a dreary life in the cold earth; the flower roots are dead, and no soft dews descend for us to drink, no little seed or leaf can we find. Ah, good Fairy, let us be your servants; give us but a few crumbs of your daily bread, and we will do all in our power to serve you."

And Violet said, "Yes;" so day after day they labored to make a pathway through the frozen earth, that she might reach the roots of the withered flowers; and soon, wherever through the dark galleries she went, the soft light fell upon the roots of the flowers, and they with new life, spread forth in the warm ground, and forced fresh sap to the blossoms above. Brightly they bloomed and danced in the soft light, and the Frost-Spirits tried in vain to harm them, for when they came beneath the bright clouds their power to do evil left them.

From his dark castle the King looked out on the happy flowers, which nodded gayly to him, and in sweet odors strove to tell him of the good little Spirit, who toiled so faithfully below, that they might live. And when turned from the brightness without, to his stately palace, it seemed so cold and dreary, that he folded Violet's mantle round

PRIMROSES.

him, and sat beneath the faded wreath upon his
ice-carved throne, wondering at the strange
warmth that came from it; till at length he bade
his Spirits bring the little Fairy from her dismal
prison.

Soon they came hastening back, and prayed
him to come and see how lovely the dark cell had
grown. The rough floor was spread with deep
green moss, and over wall and roof grew flowery
vines, filling the air with their sweet breath ; while
above played the clear, soft light, casting rosy
shadows on the fragrant leaves, and beneath the
vines stood Violet, casting crumbs to the downy
little moles who ran fearlessly about and listened
as she sang to them.

When the old King saw how much fairer she
had made the dreary cell than his palace rooms,
gentle thoughts within whispered him to grant her
prayer, and let the little Fairy go back to her
friends and home. But the Frost-Spirits breathed
upon the flowers and bid him see how frail they
were, and useless to a King. Then the stern,
cold thoughts came back again, and he harshly
bid her follow him.

With a sad farewell to her little friends she followed him, and before the throne awaited his command. When the King saw how pale and sad the gentle face had grown, how thin her robe, and weak her wings, and yet how lovingly the golden shadows fell around her and brightened as they lay upon the wand, which, guided by patient love, had made his once desolate home so bright, he could not be cruel to the one who had done so much for him, and in kindly tone said,

" Little Fairy, I offer you two things, and you may choose between them. If I will vow never more to harm the flowers you may love, will you go back to your own people and leave me and my Spirits to work our will on all the other flowers that bloom? The earth is broad, and we can find them in any land, then why should you care what happens to their kindred if your own are safe? Will you do this?"

" Ah !" answered Violet sadly, " do you not know that beneath the flowers' bright leaves there beats a little heart that loves and sorrows like our own? And can I, heedless of their beauty, doom them to pain and grief, that I might save my **own**

dear blossoms from the cruel foes to which I leave
them? Ah no! sooner would I dwell forever in
your darkest cell, than lose the love of those
warm, trusting hearts."

"Then listen," said the King, "to the task I
give you. You shall raise up for me a palace
fairer than this, and if you can work that miracle
I will grant your prayer or lose my kingly crown.
And now go forth, and begin your task; my
Spirits shall not harm you, and I will wait till it is
done before I blight another flower."

Then out into the gardens went Violet with a
heavy heart; for she had toiled so long, her
strength was nearly gone. But the flowers whispered their gratitude, and folded their leaves as if
they blessed her; and when she saw the garden
filled with loving friends, who strove to cheer and
thank her for her care, courage and strength returned; and raising up thick clouds of mist, that
hid her from the wondering flowers, alone and
trustingly she began her work.

As the time went by, the Frost-King feared the
task had been too hard for the Fairy; sounds
were heard behind the walls of mist, bright

shadows seen to pass within, but the little voice was never heard. Meanwhile the golden light had faded from the garden, the flowers bowed their heads, and all was dark and cold as when the gentle Fairy came.

And to the stern King this seemed more desolate and sad, for he missed the warm light, the happy flowers, and, more than all, the gay voice and bright face of little Violet. So he wandered through his dreary palace, wondering how he had been content to live before without sunlight and love.

And little Violet was mourned as dead in Fairy Land, and many tears were shed, for the gentle Fairy was beloved by all, from the Queen to the humblest flower. Sadly they watched over every bird and blossom which she had loved, and strove to be like her in kindly words and deeds. They wore cypress wreaths, and spoke of her as one whom they should never see again.

Thus they dwelt in deepest sorrow, till one day there came to them an unknown messenger, wrapped in a dark mantle, who looked with wondering eyes on the bright palace, and flower-

crowned Elves, who kindly welcomed him, and
brought fresh dew and rosy fruit to refresh the
weary stranger. Then he told them that he came
from the Frost-King, who begged the Queen and
all her subjects to come and see the palace little
Violet had built; for the veil of mist would soon
be withdrawn, as she could not make a fairer
home than the ice-castle, the King wished her
kindred near to comfort her and to bear her
home. And while the Elves wept, she told them
how patiently she had toiled, how her fadeless love
had made the dark cell bright and beautiful.

These and many other little things he told
them; for little Violet had won the love of many
of the Frost-Spirits, and even when they killed
the flowers she had toiled so hard to bring to
life and beauty, she spoke gentle words to
them, and sought to teach them how beautiful
is love. Long stayed the messenger, and deeper
grew his wonder that the Fairy could have left
so fair a home, to toil in the dreary palace of
his cruel master, and suffer cold and weariness,
to give life and joy to the weak and sorrowing.
When the Elves promised they would come, he

bade farewell to happy Fairy-Land, and flew sadly home.

MEALY PRIMROSE.

At last the time arrived, and out in his barren garden, under a canopy of dark clouds, sat the Frost King before the misty wall, behind which were heard low, sweet sounds, as of rustling trees and warbling birds.

Soon through the air came many-colored troops of Elves. First the Queen, known by the silver lilies on her snowy robe and the bright crown in her hair, beside whom flew a band of Elves in crimson and gold, making sweet music on their flower-trumpets, while all around, with smiling faces and bright eyes, fluttered her loving subjects.

On they came, like a flock of brilliant butterflies, their shining wings and many-colored garments sparkling in the dim air; and soon the leafless trees were gay with living flowers, and their sweet voices filled the gardens with music. Like his subjects, the King looked on the lovely Elves, and no longer wondered that the little Violet wept and longed for her home. Darker and more desolate seemed his stately home, and when the Fairies asked for flowers, he felt ashamed that he had none to give them.

At length a warm wind swept through the gardens, and the mist-clouds passed away, while in silent wonder looked the Frost King and the Elves upon the scene before them.

Far as the eye could reach were tall green trees, whose drooping boughs made graceful arches, through which the golden light shone softly, making bright shadows on the deep green moss below, where the fairest flowers waved in the cool wind, and sang, in their low, sweet voices, how beautiful is love.

Flowering vines folded their soft leaves around the trees, making green pillars of their rough trunks. Fountains threw their bright waters to the roof, and flocks of silver-winged birds flew singing among the flowers, or brooded lovingly above their nests. Doves with gentle eyes cooed among the green leaves, snow-white clouds floated in the sunny sky, and the golden light, brighter than before, shone softly down.

Soon through the long aisles came Violet, flowers and green leaves rustling as she passed. On she went to the Frost-King's throne, bearing two crowns, one of sparkling icicles, the other of pure white lilies, and kneeling before him said,

" My task is done, and, thanks to the spirits of earth and air, I have made as fair a home as Elfin hands can form. You must now decide, Will you be King of Flower Land, and own my gentle kindred for your loving friends? Will you possess unfading peace and joy, and the grateful love of all the green earth's fragrant children? Then take this crown of flowers. But if you can find no pleasure here, go back to your own cold home, and dwell in solitude and darkness, where no ray of sunlight or of joy can enter.

" Send forth your Spirits to carry sorrow and desolation over the happy earth, and win for yourself the fear and hatred of those who would so gladly love and reverence you. Then take this glittering crown, hard and cold as your own heart will be, if you will shut out all that is bright and beautiful. Both are before you. Choose."

The old King looked at the little Fairy, and saw how lovingly the bright shadows gathered round her, as if to shield her from every harm; the timid birds nestled in her bosom, and the flowers grew fairer as she looked upon them; while her gentle friends, with tears in their bright eyes, folded their hands beseechingly, and smiled on her.

Kind thoughts came thronging to his mind, and he turned to look at the two palaces. Violet's, so fair and beautiful, with rustling trees, calm, sunny skies, and happy birds and flowers, all created by her patient love and care. His own, so cold and dark and dreary, his empty gardens where no flowers could bloom, no green trees dwell, or gay birds sing, all desolate and dim ; and while he gazed, his own Spirits, casting off their dark mantles, knelt before him and besought him not to send them forth to blight the things the gentle Fairies loved so much. " We have served you long and faithfully," said they, "give us now our freedom, that we may learn to be loved by the sweet flowers we have harmed so long. Grant the little Fairy's prayer, and let her go back to her own dear home. She has taught us that Love is mightier than Fear. Choose the Flower crown, and we will be the truest subjects you have ever had."

Then, amid a burst of wild, sweet music, the Frost King placed the Flower crown on his head,

and knelt to little Violet; while far and near, over
the broad green earth, sounded the voices of the
flowers, singing their thanks to the gentle Fairy,
and the summer wind was laden with perfumes,
which they sent as tokens of their gratitude; and
wherever she went, old trees bent down to fold
their slender branches round her, flowers laid
their soft faces against her own, and whispered
blessings; even the humble moss bent over the
little feet, and kissed them as they passed.

The old King, surrounded by the happy Fairies, sat in Violet's lovely home, and watched his
icy castle melt away beneath the bright sunlight;
while his Spirits, cold and gloomy no longer,
danced with the Elves, and waited on their King
with loving eagerness. Brighter grew the golden
light, gayer sang the birds, and the harmonious
voices of grateful flowers sounding over the earth,
carried new joy to all their gentle kindred.

RIGHTER shone the golden shad-
ows;
On the cool wind softly came
The low, sweet tones of happy
flowers,
Singing little Violet's name.
'Mong the green trees was it whispered,
And the bright waves bore it on
To the lonely forest flowers,
Where the glad news had not gone.

Thus the Frost King lost his kingdom,
And his power to harm and blight;
Violet conquered, and his cold heart
Warmed the music, love, and light;
And his fair home, once so dreary,
Gay with lovely Elves and flowers,
Brought a joy that never faded
Through the long bright summer hours.

Thus, by Violet's magic power,
　　All dark shadows passed away,
And o'er the home of happy flowers
　　The golden light forever lay.
Thus the Fairy mission ended,
　　And all Flower Land was taught
The "Power of Love," by gentle deeds
　　That little Violet wrought.

As Sunny Lock ceased, another little Elf came
forward; and this was the tale "Silver Wing"
told.

Eva's
Visit to Fairy Land.

Down among the grass and
fragrant clover lay little Eva by the
brookside, watching the bright waves, as
they went singing by under the drooping
flowers that grew on its banks. As she
was wondering where the waters went,
she heard a faint, low sound, as of far-off
music. She thought it was the wind, but
not a leaf was stirring, and soon through
the rippling water came a strange little
boat.

It was a lily of the valley, whose tall stem formed the mast, while the broad leaves that rose from the roots, and dropped again till they reached the water, were filled with gay little Elves, who danced to the music of the silver lily-bells above, that rang a merry peal, and filled the air with their fragrant breath.

On came the fairy boat, till it reached a moss-grown rock; and here it stopped, while the Fairies rested beneath the violet leaves and sang with the dancing waves.

Eva looked with wonder on their gay faces and bright garments, and in the joy of her heart sang too, and threw crimson fruit for the little folks to feast upon.

They looked kindly on the child, and, after whispering among themselves, two little bright-eyed Elves flew over the shining water, and, lighting on the clover-blossoms, said gently, "Little maiden, many thanks for your kindness; and our Queen bids us ask you if you will go with us to Fairy Land, and learn what we can teach you."

"Gladly would I go with you, dear Fairies," said Eva, "but I cannot sail in your little boat.

See! I can hold you in my hand, and could not live among you without harming your tiny kingdom, I am so large."

Then the Elves laughed gayly, as they folded their arms about her, saying, "You are a good child, dear Eva, to fear doing harm to those weaker than yourself. You cannot hurt us now. Look in the water and see what we have done."

Eva looked into the brook, and saw a tiny child standing between the Elves. "Now I can go with you," said she, "but see, I can no longer step from the bank to yonder stone, for the brook seems now like a great river, and you have not given me wings like yours."

But the Fairies took each a hand, and flew lightly over the stream. The Queen and her subjects came to meet her, and all seemed glad to say some kindly word of welcome to the little stranger. They placed a flower-crown upon her head, laid their soft faces against her own, and soon it seemed as if the gentle Elves had always been her friends.

"Now must we go home," said the Queen, "and you shall go with us, little one."

Then there was a great bustle, as they flew
about on shining wing, some laying cushions of
violet leaves in the boat, others folding the
Queen's veil and mantle more closely round her,
lest the falling dews should chill her.

The cool waves' gentle splashing against the
boat, and the sweet chime of the lily-bells, lulled
little Eva to sleep, and when she was woke it was
in Fairy Land.   A faint, rosy light, as of the setting sun, shone on the white pillars of the Queen's
palace as they passed in, and the sleeping flowers
leaned gracefully on their dreaming beneath their
soft green curtains.   All was cool and still, and
the Elves glided silently about, lest they should
break their slumbers.   They led Eva to a bed of
pure white leaves, above which drooped the fragrant petals of a crimson rose.

"You can look at the bright colors till the
light fades, and then the rose will sing you to
sleep," said the Elves, as they folded the soft
leaves about her, gently kissing her, and stole
away.

Long she lay watching the bright shadows, and
listening to the song of the rose, while through

the long night dreams of lovely things floated like
bright clouds through her mind; while the rose
bent lovingly above her, and sang in the clear
moonlight.

With the sun rose the Fairies, and, with Eva,
hastened away to the fountain, whose cool waters
were soon filled with little forms, and the air ringing with happy voices, as the Elves floated in the
blue waves among the fair lilies, or sat on the
green moss, smoothing their bright locks, and
wearing garlands of dewy flowers. At length
the Queen came forth, and her subjects gathered round her and while the flowers bowed
their heads, and the trees hushed their rustling,
the Fairies sang their morning hymn to the Father
of birds and blossoms, who had made the earth
so fair a home for them.

Then they flew away to the gardens, and soon,
high up among the tree-tops, or under the broad
leaves, sat the Elves in little groups, taking their
breakfast of fruit and pure fresh dew; while the
bright-winged birds came fearlessly among them,
pecking the same ripe berries, and dipping their
little beaks in the same flower-cups, and the

Fairies folded their arms lovingly about them, smoothed their soft bosoms, and gayly sang to them.

"Now, little Eva," said they, "you will see that Fairies are not idle, wilful Spirits, as mortals believe. Come, we will show you what we do."

They led her to a lovely room, through whose walls of deep green leaves the light stole softly in. Here lay many wounded insects, and harmless little creatures, whom cruel hands had hurt; and pale, drooping flowers grew beside urns of healing herbs, from whose fresh leaves came a faint, sweet perfume.

Eva wondered, but silently followed her guide, little Rose-Leaf, who with tender words passed among the delicate blossoms, pouring dew on their feeble roots, cheering them with her loving words and happy smile.

Then she went to the insects; first to a little fly who lay in a flower-leaf cradle.

"Do you suffer much, dear Gauzy-Wing?" asked the Fairy. "I will bind up your poor little leg, and Zephyr shall rock you to sleep." So she folded the cool leaves tenderly about the poor fly, bathed his wings, and brought him refreshing drink, while he hummed his thanks, and forgot his pain, as Zephyr softly sung and fanned him with her waving wings.

They passed on, and Eva saw beside each bed a Fairy, who with gentle hands and loving words soothed the suffering insects. At length they stopped beside a bee, who lay among sweet honeysuckle flowers, in a cool, still place, where the summer wind blew in, and the green leaves rustled pleasantly. Yet he seemed to find no rest, and murmured of the pain he was doomed to bear. " Why must I lie here, while my kindred are out in the pleasant fields enjoying the sunlight and the fresh air, and cruel hands have doomed me to this dark place and bitter pain when I have done no wrong? Uncared for and forgotten, I must stay here among these poor things who think only of themselves. Come here, Rose-Leaf, and bind up my wounds, for I am far more useful than idle bird or fly."

Then said the Fairy, while she bathed the broken wing,

" Love-Blossom, you should not murmur. We

may find happiness in seeking to be patient even
while we suffer. You are not forgotten or uncared for, but others need our care more than
you, and to those who take cheerfully the pain
and sorrow sent, do we most gladly give our
help. You need not be idle, even though lying
here in darkness and sorrow ; you can be taking
from your heart all sad and discontented feelings,
and if love and patience blossom there, you will
be better for the lonely hours spent here. Look
on the bed beside you ; this little dove has suffered
far greater pain than you, and all our care can
never ease it ; yet through the long days he hath
lain here, not an unkind word or a repining sigh
hath he uttered. Ah, Love-Blossom, the gentle bird
can teach a lesson you will be wise and better for."

Then a faint voice whispered, "Little Rose-
Leaf, come quickly, or I cannot thank you as I
ought for all your loving care for me."

So they passed to the bed beside the discontented bee, and here upon the softest down lay
the dove, whose eyes looked gratefully upon the
Fairy, as she knelt beside the little couch,
smoothed the soft white bosom, folded her arms

about it and wept sorrowing tears, while the bird still whispered its gratitude and love.

"Dear Fairy, the fairest flowers have cheered me with their sweet breath, fresh dew and fragrant leaves have been ready for me, gentle hands to tend, kindly hearts to love; and for this I can only thank you and say farewell."

Then the quivering wings were still, and the patient little dove was dead; but the bee murmured no longer, and the dew from the flowers fell like tears around the quiet bed.

Sadly Rose-Leaf led Eva away, saying, "Lily-Bosom shall have a grave to-night beneath our fairest blossoms, and you shall see that gentleness and love are prized far above gold or beauty, here in Fairy Land. Come now to the Flower Palace, and see the Fairy Court."

Beneath green arches, bright with birds and flowers, beside singing waves, went Eva into a lofty hall. The roof of pure white lilies rested on pillars of green clustering vines, while many-colored blossoms threw their bright shadows on the walls, as they danced below in the deep green moss, and their low, sweet voice sounded softly through the sunlit palace, while the rustling leaves kept time.

Beside the throne stood Eva, and watched the lovely forms around her, as they stood, each little band in its own color, with glistening wings, and flower wands.

Suddenly the music grew louder and sweeter, and the Fairies knelt, and bowed their heads, as on through the crowd of loving subjects came the Queen, while the air was filled with gay voices singing to welcome her.

She placed the child beside her, saying, "Little Eva, you shall see now how the flowers on your great earth bloom so brightly. A band of loving little gardeners go daily forth from Fairy Land, to tend and watch them, that no harm may befall the gentle spirits that dwell beneath their leaves. This is never known, for like all good it is unseen by mortal eyes, and unto only pure hearts like yours do we make known our secret. The humblest flower that grows is visited by our messengers, and often blooms in fragrant beauty, unknown, unloved by all save Fairy friends, who seek to fill the spirits with all sweet and gentle virtues, that they may not be useless on the earth;

for the noblest mortals stoop to learn of flowers.
Now, Eglantine, what have you to tell us of your
rosy namesakes on the earth?"

From a group of Elves, whose rose-wreathed
wands showed the flower they loved, came one
bearing a tiny urn, answering the Queen, she said:

"Over hill and valley they are blooming fresh
and fair as summer sun and dew can make them.
No drooping stem or withered leaf tell of any evil
thought within their fragrant bosoms, and thus
from the fairest of their race have they gathered
this sweet dew, as a token of their gratitude to
one whose tenderness and care have kept them
pure and happy; and this, the loveliest of their
sisters, have I brought to place among the Fairy
flowers that never pass away."

Eglantine laid the urn before the Queen, and
placed the fragrant rose on the dewy moss beside
the throne, while the murmur of approval went
through the hall, as each elfin wand waved to the
little Fairy who had toiled so well and faithfully,
and could bring so fair a gift to their good
Queen.

Then came forth an Elf bearing a withered

leaf, while her many-colored robe and purple tulips in her hair told her name and charge.

"Dear Queen," she sadly said, "I would gladly bring as pleasant tidings as my sister, but, alas! my flowers are proud and wilful, and when I went to gather my little gift of colored leaves for royal garments, they bade me bring this withered blossom and tell you they would serve no longer one who will not make them Queen over all the other flowers. They would yield neither dew or honey, but proudly closed their leaves and bid me go."

"Your task has been too hard for you," said the Queen kindly, as she place the drooping flower in the urn Eglantine had given, "you will see how this dew from a sweet, pure heart will give new life and loveliness even to this poor faded one. So can you, dear Rainbow, by loving words and gentle teachings, bring back lost purity and peace to those whom pride and selfishness have blighted. Go once again to the proud flowers, and tell them when they are queen of their own hearts they will ask no fairer kingdom. Watch more tenderly than ever over them, see that they

lack neither dew nor air, speak lovingly to them,
and let no unkind word or deed of theirs anger
you.   Let them see by your patient love and care
how much fairer they might be, and when next
you come, you will be laden with gifts from humble, loving flowers."

Thus they told what they had done, and received from their Queen some gentle chiding or
loving word of praise.

"You will be weary of this," said little Rose-
Leaf to Eva ; "come now and see where we are
taught to read the tales written on flower-leaves,
and the sweet language of the birds, and all that
make a Fairy heart wiser and better."

Then into a cheerful place they went, where
were many groups of flowers, among whose
leaves sat the child Elves, and learned from their
flower-books all that Fairy hands had written
there.   Some studied how to watch the tender
buds, when to spread them to the sunlight, and
when to shelter them from rain ; how to guard the
ripening seeds, and when to lay them in the warm
earth or send them on the summer wind to far-off
hills and valleys, where other Fairy hands would

Flower Fables—4

tend and cherish them, till a sisterhood of happy flowers spring up to beautify and gladden the lonely spot where they had fallen. Others learn to heal the wounded insects, whose frail limbs a breeze could shatter, and who, were it not for the Fairy hands, die, ere their happy summer life had gone. Some learned how by pleasant dreams to cheer and comfort mortal hearts, by whispered words of love to save from evil deeds those who had gone astray, to fill young hearts with gentle thoughts and pure affections, that no sign might mar the beauty of the human flower; while others, like mortal children, learned the Fairy alphabet. Thus the Elves made loving friends by care and love, and no evil thing could harm them, for those they helped to cherish and protect ever watched to shield and save them.

Eva nodded to the gay little ones, as they peeped from among the leaves at the stranger, and then she listened to the Fairy lessons. Several tiny Elves stood on a broad leaf while the teacher sat among the petals of a flower that bent

cowslips.

beside them, and asked questions that none but Fairies would care to know.

"Twinkle, if there lay nine seeds within a flower-cup and the wind bore five away, how many would the blossom have?"

"Four," replied the little one.

"Rosebud, if a cowslip opens three leaves in one day and four the next, how many rosy leaves will there be when the whole flower has bloomed?"

"Seven," sang the gay little Elf.

"Harebell, if a silk worm spin one yard of Fairy cloth in an hour, how many will it spin in a day."

"Twelve," said the Fairy child.

"Primrose, where lies Violet Island?"

"In the Lake of Ripples."

"Lilla, you may bound Rose-Land."

"On the north by Ferndale, south by Sunny Wave River, east by the hill of Morning Clouds, and west by the Evening Star."

"Now, little ones," said the teacher, "you go to your painting, that our visitor may see how we repair the flowers that earthly hands have injured."

Then Eva saw how on large, white leaves, the

Fairies learned to imitate the lovely colors, and with tiny brushes to brighten the blush on the anemone's cheek, to deepen the blue of the Violet's eye, and add new light to the golden cowslip.

"You have stayed long enough," said the Elves at length, "we have many things to show you. Come now and see what is our dearest work."

So Eva said farewell to the child Elves, and hastened with little Rose-Leaf to the gates. Here she saw many bands of Fairies, folded in dark mantles that mortals might not know them, who, with the child among them, flew away over hill and valley. Some went to the cottages amid the hills, some to the seaside to watch above the humble fisher folks; but little Rose-Leaf and many others went into the noisy city.

Eva wondered within herself what good the tiny Elves could do in this great place; but she soon learned, for the Fairy band went among the poor and friendless, bringing pleasant dreams to the sick and old, sweet, tender thoughts of love and gentleness to the young, strength to the weak, and patient cheerfulness to the poor and lonely.

Then the child wondered no longer, but deeper grew her love for the tender-hearted Elves, who left their own happy home to cheer and comfort those who never knew what hands had clothed and fed them, what hearts had given of their own joy, and brought such happiness to theirs.

Long they stayed, and many a lesson little Eva learned ; but when she begged them to go back, they still led her on, saying, "Our work is not yet done ; shall we leave so many sad hearts when we may cheer them, so many dark homes that we may brighten ? We must stay yet longer, little Eva, and you may learn yet more."

Then they went into a dark and lonely room, and where they found a pale, sad-eyed child, who wept bitter tears over a faded flower.

"Ah," sighed the little one, "it was my only friend, and I cherished it with all my heart's love ; 'twas all that made my sad life happy ; and it is gone."

Tenderly the child fastened the drooping stem, and placed it where the one faint ray of sunlight stole into the room.

"Do you see," said the Elves, "through this simple flower will we keep the child pure and stainless amid the sin and sorrow around her. The love of this shall lead her on through temptation and through grief, and she shall be a spirit of joy and consolation to the sinful and sorrowing."

And with busy love toiled the Elves amid the withered leaves, and new strength was given to the flower; while, as day by day the friendless child watched the growing buds, deeper grew her love for the unseen friends who had given her one thing to cherish in her lonely home; sweet, gentle thoughts filled her heart as she bent above it, and the blossom's fragrant breath was to her a whispered voice of all fair and lovely things, and as the flower taught her, so she taught others.

The loving Elves brought her sweet dreams by night, and happy thoughts by day, and as she grew in childlike beauty, pure and patient amid poverty and sorrow, the sinful were rebuked, sorrowing hearts grew light, and the weak and selfish forgot their idle fears, when they saw her trustingly live on with none to aid or comfort her. The

love she bore the tender flower kept her own
heart innocent and bright, and the pure human
flower was a lesson to those who looked upon it;
and soon the gloomy house was bright with happy
hearts, that learned of a gentle child to bear pov
erty and grief as she had done, to forgive those
who brought care and wrong to them, and to seek
for happiness in humble deeds of charity and love.

"Our work is done," whispered the Elves, and
with blessings on the two fair flowers, they flew
away to other homes;—to a blind old man who
dwelt alone with none to love him, till through
long years of darkness and of silent sorrow the
heart within had grown dim and cold. No sunlight could enter at the darkened eyes, and none
were near to whisper gentle words, to cheer and
comfort.

Thus he dwelt forgotten and alone, seeking to
give no joy to others, possessing none himself.
Life was dark and sad till the untiring Elves came
to his dreary home, bringing sunlight and love.
They whispered sweet words of comfort—how, if
the darkened eyes could find no light without,
within there might be never-failing happiness;

gentle feelings and sweet, loving thoughts could
make the heart fair, if the gloomy, selfish sorrow
were but cast away, and all would be bright and
beautiful.

They brought light-hearted children, who gathered round him, making the desolate home fair
with their young faces, and his sad heart gay
with their sweet, childish voices. The love they
bore he could not cast away, sunlight stole in, the
dark thoughts passed away, and the earth was a
pleasant home for him.

Thus their little hands led him back to peace
and happiness, flowers bloomed beside his door,
and their fragrant breath brought happy thoughts
of pleasant valleys and green hills ; birds sang to
him, and their sweet voices woke the music in his
soul, that never failed to calm and comfort.
Happy sounds were heard in his once lonely
home, and bright faces gathered round his knee.
and listened tenderly while he strove to tell them
all the good that gentleness and love had done
for him.

Still the Elves watched near, and brighter
grew the heart as kindly thoughts and tender

feelings entered in, and made it their home, and
when the old man fell asleep, above his grave
little feet trod lightly, and loving hands laid fragrant flowers.

Then went the Elves into dreary prison-houses,
where sad hearts pined in lonely sorrow for the
joy and freedom they had lost. To these came
the loving band with tender words, telling of the
peace they might yet win by patient striving and
repentant tears, thus waking in their bosoms all
the holy feelings and sweet affections that had
slept so long.

They told pleasant tales, and sang their sweetest songs to cheer and gladden, while the dim
cells grew bright with the sunlight, and fragrant
flowers the loving Elves had brought, and by their
gentle teachings those sad, despairing hearts
were filled with patient hope and earnest longing
to win back their lost innocence and joy.

Thus to all who needed help or comfort went
faithful Fairies, and when at length they turned
towards Fairy Land, many were the grateful,
happy hearts they left behind.

Then through the summer sky, above the

blossoming earth, they journeyed home, happier for the joy they had given, wiser for the good they had done.

All Fairy Land was dressed in flowers, and the soft wind went sighing by, laden with their fragrant breath. Sweet music sounded through the air, and troops of Elves in their gayest robes hastened to the palace where the feast was spread.

Soon the bright hall was filled with smiling faces and fair forms, and little Eva, as she stood beside the Queen, thought she had never seen a sight so lovely.

The many-colored shadows of the fairest flowers played on the white walls, and fountains sparkled in the sunlight, making music as the cool waves rose and fell, while two and fro with waving wings and joyous voices, went the smiling Elves, bearing fruit and honey, or fragrant garlands for each other's hair.

Long they feasted, gayly they sang, and Eva danced merrily among them, longed to be an Elf that she might dwell forever in so fair a home.

At length the music ceased, and the Queen

said, as she laid her hand on little Eva's shining hair :

"Dear child, to-morrow we must bear you home, for, much as we long to keep you, it were wrong to bring such sorrow to your loving earthly friends ; therefore we will guide you to the brook-side, and there say farewell till you come again to visit us. Nay, do not weep, dear Rose-Leaf ; you shall watch over little Eva's flowers, and when she looks at them she will think of you. Come now and lead her to the Fairy garden, and show her what we think our fairest sight. Weep no more, but strive to make her last hours with us happy as you can."

With gentle caresses and most tender words the loving Elves gathered about the child, and, with Rose-Leaf by her side, they led her through the palace, and along green, winding paths, till Eva saw what seemed a wall of flowers rising before her, while the air was filled with the most fragrant odors, and low, sweet music as of singing blossoms.

"Where have you brought me, and what mean these lovely sounds?" asked Eva.

THERE CAME A STRANGE LITTLE BOAT FILLED WITH ELVES.

"Look here, and you shall see," said Rose Leaf, as she bent aside the vines, "but listen silently or you cannot hear."

Then Eva, looking through the drooping vines, beheld a garden filled with the loveliest flowers ; fair as were all the blossoms she had seen in Fairy Land, none were so beautiful as these. The rose glowed with a deeper crimson, the lily's soft leaves were more purely white, the crocus and humble cowslip shone like sunlight, and the violet was blue as the sky that smiled above it.

"How beautiful they are," whispered Eva, "but, dear Rose-Leaf, why do you keep them here, and why call you this your fairest sight?"

"Look again, and I will tell you," answered the Fairy.

Eva looked, and saw from every flower a tiny form come forth to welcome the Elves who all, save Rose-Leaf had flown above the wall, and were now scattering dew upon the flowers' bright leaves and talking gayly with the Spirits, who gathered round them, and seemed full of joy that they had come. The child saw that each one wore the

colors of the flower that was its home.   Delicate
and graceful were the little forms, bright the
silken hair that fell about each lovely face; and
Eva heard the low, sweet murmur of their silvery
voices and the rustle of their wings.   She gazed
in silent wonder, forgetting she knew not who
they were till the Fairy said,

" These are the spirits of the flowers, and this
the Fairy Home where those whose hearts were
pure and loving on the earth come to bloom in
fadeless beauty here, when their earthly life is
past.   The humblest flower that blooms has a
home with us, for outward beauty is a worthless
thing if all be not fair and sweet within.   Do you
see yonder lovely spirit singing with my sister
Moonlight? a clover blossom was her home, and
she dwelt unknown, unloved; yet patient and
content, bearing cheerfully the sorrows sent her.
We watched and saw how fair and sweet the
humble flower grew, and then gladly bore her
here, to blossom with the lily and the rose.   The
flowers' lives are often short, for cruel hands destroy them; therefore is it our greatest joy to
bring them hither, where no careless foot or wintry

wind can harm them, where they bloom in quiet
beauty, repaying our care by their love and sweetest perfumes?"

"I will never break another flower," cried Eva;
"but let me go to them, dear Fairy; I would
gladly know the lovely spirits, and ask forgiveness
for the sorrow I have caused. May I not go in?"

"Nay, dear Eva, you are a mortal child, and
cannot enter here; but I will tell them of the kind
maiden who has learned to love them, and they
will remember you when you have gone. Come
now, for you have seen enough, and we must be
away."

On a rosy morning cloud, surrounded by the
loving Elves, went Eva through the sunny sky.
The fresh wind bore them gently on, and soon
they stood again beside the brook, whose waves
danced brightly as if to welcome them.

"Now, ere we say farewell," said the Queen,
as they gathered nearer to the child, "tell me,
dear Eva, what among all our Fairy gifts will
make you happiest, and it shall be yours."

"You good little Fairies," said Eva, folding
them in her arms, for she was no longer the tiny

child she had been in Fairy Land, "you dear good little Elves, what can I ask of you, who have done so much to make me happy, and taught me so many good and gentle lessons, the memory of which will never pass away? I can only ask of you the power to be as pure and gentle as yourselves, as tender and loving to the weak and sorrowing, as untiring in kindly deeds to all. Grant me this gift, and you shall see that little Eva has not forgotten what you have taught her."

"The power is yours," said the Elves, and laid their soft hands on her head; we will watch over you in dreams, and when you would have tidings of us, ask the flowers in your garden, and they will tell you all you would know. Farewell. Remember Fairy Land and all your loving friends."

They clung about her tenderly, and little Rose-Leaf placed a flower crown on her head, whispering softly, "When you would come to us again, stand by the brook-side and wave this in the air, and we will gladly take you to our home again. Farewell, dear Eva. Think of your little Rose-Leaf when among the flowers."

Flower Fables—5

Long Eva watched their shining wings. and listened to the music of their voices as they flew singing home, and when at length the last little form had vanished among the clouds, she saw that all around here where the Elves had been, the fairest flowers had sprung up, and the lonely brook-side was a blooming garden.

Thus she stood among the waving blossoms, with the Fairy garland in her hair, and happy feelings in her heart, better and wiser for her visit to Fairy Land.

"Now, Star-Twinkle, what have you to teach?" asked the Queen.

"Nothing but a little song I heard the hare-bells singing," replied the Fairy, and, taking her harp, sang, in a low, sweet voice,

The Flower's Lesson.

HERE grew a fragrant rose-tree
    where the brook flows,
  With two little tender buds, and
    one full rose ;
  When the sun went down to his
    bed in the west,
The little buds leaned on the rose-mother's breast,
While the bright-eyed stars their long watch kept,
And the flowers of the valley in their green
  cradles slept ;
Then silently in odors they communed with each
  other,
The two little buds on the bosom of their mother.
"O sister," said the little one, as she gazed at the
  sky,

"I wish that the Dew Elves, as they wander
lightly by,
Would bring me a star; for they never grow dim,
And the Father does not need them to burn
around him.
The shining drops of dew the Elves bring each
day
And place in my bosom, so soon pass away;
But a star would glitter brightly through the long
summer hours
And I should be fairer than all my sister flowers.
That were better far than the dew-drops that fall
On the high and the low, and come alike to all.
I would be fair and stately, with a bright star to
shine
And give a queenly air to this crimson robe of
mine."
And proudly she cried, "These fire-flies shall be
My jewels, since the stars can never come to me."
Just then a tiny dew-drop that hung o'er the dell
On the breast of the bud like a soft star fell;
But impatiently she flung it away from her leaf,

And it fell on her mother like a tear of grief,
While she folded to her breast, with wilful pride,
A glittering fire-fly that hung by her side.
"Heed," said the mother-rose, "daughter mine,
Why should thou seek for beauty not thine?
The Father hath made thee what thou now art;
And what he most loveth is a sweet, pure heart.
Then why dost thou take with such discontent
The loving gift which He to thee hath sent?
For the cool fresh dew will render thee far
More lovely and sweet than the brightest star;
They were made for Heaven, and can never come
    to shine
Like the fire-fly thou hast in that foolish breast of
    thine.
O my foolish little bud, do listen to thy mother;
Care only for true beauty, and seek for no other.
There will be grief and trouble in that wilful little
    heart;
Unfold thy leaves, my daughter, and let the fly
    depart."
But the proud little bud would have her own will.

And folded the fire-fly more closely still ;
Till the struggling insect tore open its vest
Of purple and green, that covered her breast.
When the sun came up, she saw with grief
The blooming of her sister bud leaf by leaf.
While she, once as fair and bright as the rest,
Hung her weary head down on her wounded
    breast.
Bright grew the sunshine, and the soft summer air
Was filled with music of flowers singing there ;
But faint grew the little bud with thirst and pain;
And longed for the cool dew ; but now 'twas in
    vain.
Then bitterly she wept for her folly and pride,
As drooping she stood by her fair sister's side.
Then the rose-mother leaned the weary little
    head
On her bosom to rest, and tenderly she said :
" Thou hast learned, my little bud, that, whatever
    may betide,

Thou canst win thyself no joy by passion or by
    pride.

The loving Father sends the sunshine and the
    shower,

That thou mayst become a perfect little flower ;

The sweet dews to feed thee, the soft wind to
    cheer.

And the earth as a pleasant home, while thou art
    dwelling here.

Then shouldst thou not be grateful for all this
    kindly care,

And strive to keep thyself most innocent and fair ?

Then seek, my little blossom, to win humility ;

Be fair without, be pure within, and thou wilt
    happy be.

So when the quiet Autumn of thy fragrant life
    shall come,

Thou mayst pass away, to bloom in the Flower
    Spirits' home."

Then from the mother's breast, where it still lay
    hid,

Into the fading bud the dewdrop gently slid ;

Stronger grew the little form, and happy tears fell,
As the dew did its silent work, and the bud grew
  well,
While the gentle rose leaned, with motherly pride,
O'er the fair little ones that bloomed at her side.
Night came again, and the fire-flies flew ;
But the bud let them pass, and drank of the
  dew,
While the soft stars shone, from the still summer
  heaven,
On the happy little flower that had learned the
  lesson given.

The music-loving Elves clapped their hands, as
Star Twinkle ceased ; and the Queen placed a
flower crown, with a gentle smile, upon the Fairy's
head, saying,

" The little bud's lesson shall teach us how sad
a thing is pride, and that humility alone can bring
true happiness to flower and Fairy. You shall
come next, Zephyr."

And the little Fairy, who lay rocking to and fro upon a fluttering vine-leaf, thus began her story :

"As I lay resting in the bosom of a cowslip that bent above the brook, a little wind, tired of play, told me this tale of

Lily-Bell and the Thistledown.

Once upon a time, two little fairies went out into the world, to seek their fortune. Thistledown was as gay and gallant a little Elf as ever spread a wing. His purple mantle, and doublet of green, were embroidered with the brightest threads, and the plume in his cap came always from the wing of the gayest butterfly.

But he was not loved in Fairy Land, for, like the flower whose name

and colors he wore, though fair to look upon,
many were the little thorns of cruelty and selfishness that lay concealed by his gay mantle. Many
a gentle flower and harmless bird died by his
hand, for he cared for himself alone, and whatever
gave him pleasure must be his, though happy
hearts were rendered sad, and peaceful homes
destroyed.

Such was Thistledown; but far different was
his little friend, Lily-Bell. Kind, compassionate,
and loving, wherever her gentle face was seen,
joy and gratitude were found; no suffering flower
or insect, that did not love and bless the kindly
Fairy; and thus all Elf Land looked upon her as a
friend.

Nor did this make her vain and heedless of
others; she humbly dwelt among them, seeking
to do all the good she might; and many a house-
less bird and hungry insect that Thistledown had
harmed did she feed and shelter, and in return no
evil could befall her, for so many friends were all
about her, seeking to repay her tenderness and
love by their watchful care.

She would not now have left Fairy Land, but

to help and counsel her wild companion, Thistledown, who, discontented with his quiet home,
would seek his fortune in the great world, and she
feared he would suffer from his own faults, for
others would not always be as gentle and forgiving as his kindred. So the kind little Fairy left her
home and friends to go with him ; and thus, side
by side, they flew beneath the bright summer sky.

On and on, over hill and valley, they went,
chasing the gay butterflies, or listening to the
bees, as they flew from flower to flower like busy
little housewives, singing as they worked ; till at
last they reached a pleasant garden, filled with
flowers and green, old trees.

"See," cried thistledown, "what a lovely home
is here ; let us rest among the cool leaves, and hear
the flowers sing, for I am sadly tired and hungry."

So into the quiet garden they went, and the
winds gayly welcomed them, while the flowers
nodded on their stems, offering their bright leaves
for the Elves to rest upon, and fresh, sweet honey
to refresh them.

"Now, dear thistle, do not harm these friendly
blossoms," said Lily-Bell ; "see how kindly they

spread their leaves, and offer us their dew. It
would be very wrong in you to repay their care

with cruelty and pain. You will be tender for my
sake, dear Thistle."

Then she went among the flowers, and they bent lovingly before her, and laid their soft leaves against her little face, that she might see how glad they were to welcome one so good and gentle, and kindly offered their dew and honey to the weary little Fairy, who sat among their fragrant petals and looked smilingly on the happy blossoms, who, with their soft, low voices, sang her to sleep.

While Lily-Bell lay dreaming among the rose-leaves, Thistledown went wandering through the garden. First he robbed the bees of their honey, and rudely shook the little flowers, that he might get the dew they had gathered to bathe their buds in. Then he chased the bright winged flies, and wounded them with the sharp thorn he carried for a sword; he broke the spider's shining webs, lamed the birds, and soon wherever he passed lay wounded insects and drooping flowers; while the winds carried the tidings over the garden, and bird and blossom looked upon him as an evil spirit, and fled away or closed their leaves, lest he should harm them.

Thus he went, leaving sorrow and pain behind him, till he came to the roses where Lily-Bell lay sleeping. There, weary of his cruel sport, he stayed to rest beneath a graceful rose-tree, where grew one blooming flower and a tiny bud.

"Why are you so slow in blooming, little one? You are too old to be rocked in your green cradle longer, and should be out among your sister flowers," said Thistle, as he lay idly in the shadow of the tree.

"My little bud is not yet strong enough to venture forth," replied the rose, as she bent fondly over it; "the sunlight and the rain would blight her tender form, were she to blossom now, but soon she will be fit to bear them; till then she is content to rest beside her mother, and to wait."

"You silly flower," said Thistledown, "see how quickly I will make you bloom! your waiting is useless." And speaking thus, he pulled rudely apart the folded leaves, and laid them open to the sun and air; while the rose mother implored the cruel Fairy to leave her little bud untouched.

"It is my first, my only one," said she, "and I have watched over it with such care, hoping it would soon bloom beside me; and now you have

destroyed it. How could you have harmed the
little helpless one, that never did aught to injure
you?" And while her tears fell like summer
rain, she drooped in grief above her little bud,
and sadly watched it fading in the sunlight; but
the Thistledown, heedless of the sorrow he had
given, spread his wings and flew away.

Soon the sky grew dark, and heavy drops
began to fall. Then Thistle hastened to the lily,
for her cup was deep, and the white leaves fell
like curtains over the fragrant bed; he was a
dainty little Elf, and could not sleep among the
clovers and bright buttercups. But when he
asked the flower to unfold her leaves and take
him in, she turned her pale, soft face away,
and answered sadly, "I must shield my little
drooping sisters whom you have harmed, and
cannot let you in."

Then Thistle was very angry, and turned to
find shelter among the stately roses; but they
showed their sharp thorns, and, while their rosy
faces glowed with anger, told him to begone, or
they would repay him for the wrong he had
done their gentle kindred.

He would have stayed to harm them, but the rain fell fast, and he hurried away, saying, "The tulips will take me in, for I have praised their beauty, and they are vain, foolish flowers."

But when he came, all wet and cold, praying for shelter among their thick leaves, they only laughed, and said scornfully, "We know you, and will not let you in, for you are false and cruel, and will only bring us sorrow. You need not come to us for another mantle, when the rain has spoiled your fine one; and do not stay here, or we will do you harm."

Then they waved their broad leaves stormily, and scattered the heavy drops on his dripping garments.

"Now must I go to the humble daisies and blue violets," said Thistle, "they will be glad to let in so fine a Fairy, and I shall die in this cold wind and rain."

So away he flew, as fast as his heavy wings would bear him, to the daisies; but they nodded their heads wisely, and closed their leaves yet closer, saying sharply,

"Go away with yourself, and do not imagine

that we will open our leaves to you, and spoil our seeds by letting in the rain. It serves you rightly; to gain our love and confidence, and repay it by such cruelty! You will find no shelter here for one whose careless hand wounded our little friend Violet, and broke the truest heart that ever beat in a flower's breast. We are very angry with you, wicked Fairy; go away and hide yourself."

"Ah," cried the shivering Elf, "where can I find shelter? I will go to the violets: they will forgive me and take me in."

But the daisies had spoken truly; the gentle little flower was dead, and her blue-eyed sisters were weeping over her faded leaves.

"Now I have no friends," sighed poor Thistle-down, "and must die of cold. Ah, if I had but minded Lily-Bell, I might be dreaming beneath some flower's leaves."

"Others can forgive and love, beside Lily-Bell and Violet," said a faint, sweet voice; "I have no little bud to shelter now, and you can enter here." It was the rose mother that spoke, and Thistle saw how pale the bright leaves had grown, and how the slender stem was bowed. Grieved.

ashamed, and wondering at the flower's forgiving
words, he laid his weary head on the bosom he
had filled with sorrow, and the fragrant leaves
were folded carefully about him.

But he could find no rest.   The rose strove to
comfort him ; but when she fancied he was sleeping, thoughts of her lost bud stole in, and the little
heart beat so sadly where he lay, that no sleep
came ; while the bitter tears he had caused to
flow fell more coldly on him than the rain without.
Then he heard the other flowers whispering among
themselves of his cruelty, and the sorrow he had
brought to their happy home ; and many wondered how the rose, who had suffered most, could
yet forgive and shelter him.

"Never could I forgive one who had robbed
me of my children.   I could bow my head and
die, but could give no happiness to one who had
taken all my own," said Hyacinth, bending fondly
over the little ones that blossomed by her side.

"Dear Violet is not the only one that will leave
us," sobbed Mignonette ; "the rose mother will
fade like her little bud, and we shall lose our gentlest teacher.   Her last lesson is forgiveness ; let

us show our love for her, and the gentle stranger Lily-Bell, by allowing no unkind word or thought of him who brought us all this grief."

The angry words were hushed, and through the long night nothing was heard but the dropping of the rain, and the low sighs of the rose.

Soon the sunlight came again, and with it Lily-Bell; but he was ashamed, and stole away.

When the flowers told their sorrow to kind-hearted Lily-Bell, she wept bitterly at the pain her friend had given, and with loving words strove to comfort those whom he had grieved; with gentle care she healed the wounded birds, and watched above the flowers he had harmed, bringing each day dew and sunlight to refresh and strengthen, till all were well again; and though sorrowing for their dead friends, still they forgave Thistle for the sake of her who had done so much for them. Thus, ere long, buds fairer than that she had lost lay on the rose mother's breast, and for all she had suffered she was well repaid by the love of Lily-Bell and her sister flowers.

And when bird, bee, and blossom were strong and fair again the gentle Fairy said farewell, and

flew away to seek her friend, leaving behind
many grateful hearts, who owed their joy and life
to her.

Meanwhile, over hill and dale went Thistledown, and for a time was kind and gentle to
every living thing. He missed sadly the little
friend who had left her happy home to watch
over him, but he was too proud to his own fault,
and so went on, hoping she would find him.

One day he fell asleep, and when he awoke
the sun had set, and the dew began to fall; the
flower-cups were closed, and he had nowhere to
go, till a friendly little bee, belated by his heavy
load of honey, bid the weary Fairy come with
him.

"Help me to bear my honey home, and you
can stay with us to-night," he kindly said.

So the Thistle gladly went with him, and soon
they came to a pleasant garden, where among
the fairest flowers stood the hive, covered with
vines and overhung with blossoming trees.
Glow-worms stood at the door to light them
home, and as they passed in, the Fairy thought
how charming it must be to dwell in such a lovely

place.   The floor of wax was pure and white as marble, while the walls were formed of golden honey-comb, and the air was fragrant with the breath of flowers.

" You cannot see our Queen to-night," said the little bee, " but I will show you a bed where you can rest."

And he led the tired Fairy to a little cell, where on a bed of flowers he folded his wings and fell asleep.

As the first ray of sunlight stole in he was awakened by sweet music.   It was the morning song of the bees.

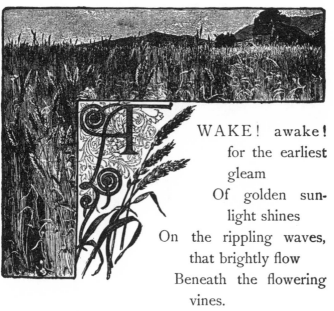

WAKE! awake!
for the earliest
gleam
Of golden sun-
light shines
On the rippling waves,
that brightly flow
Beneath the flowering
vines.
Awake! awake! for the low, sweet chant
Of the wild-birds' morning hymn
Comes floating by on the fragrant air,
Through the forest cool and dim;

Then spread each wing,
And work, and sing,

Through the long, bright sunny **hours**;
  O'er the pleasant earth
  We journey forth,
For a day among the flowers.

Awake! awake! for the summer **wind**
  Hath bidden the blossoms unclose,
Hath opened the violet's soft blue eye,
  And wakened the sleeping rose.
And lightly they wave on their slender stems
  Fragrant, and fresh, and fair,
Waiting for us, as we singing come
  To gather our honey-dew there.
    Then spread each wing,
    And work, and sing,
Through the long, bright sunny hours;
  O'er the pleasant earth
  We journey forth,
For a day among the flowers."

Soon his friend came to bid him rise, as the
Queen desired to speak with him. So, with his
purple mantle thrown gracefully over his shoulder,
and his little cap held respectfully in his hand, he
followed Nimble-Wing to the great hall, where
the Queen was being served by her pages. Some
bore her fresh dew and honey, some fanned her
with fragrant flower-leaves, while others scattered
the sweetest perfumes on the air.

"Little Fairy," said the Queen, "you are welcome to my palace; and we will gladly have you
stay with us, if you will obey our laws. We do
not spend the pleasant summer days in idleness
and pleasure, but each one labors for the happiness and good of all. If our home is beautiful,
we have made it so by industry; and here, as one
large, loving family, we dwell; no sorrow, care, or
discord can enter in while all obey the voice of
her who seeks to be wise and gentle Queen to
them. If you will stay with us, we will teach you
many things. Order, patience, industry, who can
teach so well as they who are emblems of these
virtues?

"Our laws are few and simple. You must

each day gather your share of honey, see that
your cell is sweet and fresh, as you yourself
must be ; rise with the sun, and with him to sleep.
You must harm no flower in doing your work,
nor take more than your just share of honey ; for
they so kindly give us food, it were most cruel
to treat them with aught save gentleness and
gratitude.   Now will you stay with us, and learn
what even mortal seek to know, that labor brings
true happiness ?

And Thistle said he would stay and dwell
with them ; for he was tired of wandering alone,
and thought he might live here till Lily-Bell should
come, or till he was weary of the kind-hearted
bees.   Then they took away his gay garments,
and dressed him like themselves, in the black
velvet cloak with golden bands across his breast.

"Now come with us," they said. So forth into
the green fields they went, and made their breakfast among the dewy flowers ; and then till the
sun set they flew from bud to blossom, singing
as they went, and Thistle for a while was happier
than when breaking flowers and harming gentle
birds.

But soon he grew tired of working all day in the sun, and longed to be free again. He could find no pleasure with the industrious bees, and sighed to be away with his idle friends, the butterflies, so while the others worked he slept or played, and then, in haste to get his share, he tore the flowers, and took all they had saved for their own food. Nor was this all; he told such pleasant tales of the life he led before he came to live with them, that many grew unhappy and discontented, and they who had before wished no greater joy than the love and praise of their kind Queen, now disobeyed and blamed her for all she had done to them.

Long she bore their unkind words and deeds; and when at length she found it was the ungrateful Fairy who had wrought all this trouble in her quiet kingdom, she strove, with sweet, forgiving words, to show him all the wrong he had done; but he would not listen, and still went on destroying the happiness of those who had done so much for him.

Then, when she saw that no kindness could touch his heart, she said

"Thistledown, we took you in, a friendless stranger, fed and clothed you, and made our home as pleasant to you as we could; and in return for all our care, you have brought discontent and trouble to my subjects, grief and care to me. I cannot let my peaceful kingdom be disturbed by you; therefore go and seek another home. You may find other friends, but none will love you more than we, had you been worthy of it; so farewell." And the doors of the once happy home he had disturbed were closed behind him.

Then he was very angry, and determined to bring some great sorrow on the good Queen. So he sought out the idle, wilful bees, whom he had first made discontented, bidding them follow him, and win the honey the Queen had stored up for the winter.

"Let us feast and make merry in the pleasant summer time," said Thistle; "winter is far off, why should we waste these lovely days, toiling to lay up the food we might enjoy now. Come, we will take what we have made, and think no more of what the Queen has said."

So while the industrious bees were out among

THISTLEDOWN VISITS THE QUEEN BEE.

the flowers, he led the drones to the hive, and took possession of the honey, destroying and laying waste the home of the kind bees ; then, fearing that in their grief and anger they might harm him, Thistle flew away to make new friends.

After many wanderings, he came at length to a great forest, and here beside a still lake he stayed to rest. Delicate wood-flowers grew near him in the deep green moss, with drooping heads, as if they listened to the soft wind sighing among the pines. Bright-eyed birds peeped at him from their nests, and many-colored insects danced above the cool, still lake.

"This is a pleasant place," said Thistle ; "it shall be my home for a while. Come hither, blue dragon-fly, I would gladly make a friend of you, for I am all alone."

The dragon-fly folded his shining wings beside the Elf, listened to the tale he told, promised to befriend the lonely one, and strove to make the forest a happy home for him.

So here dwelt Thistle, and many kind friends gathered around him, for he spoke gently to them, and they knew nothing of the cruel deeds he had done; and for a while he was happy and content. But at length he grew weary of the gentle birds and wild-flowers, and sought new pleasure in destroying the beauty he was tired of; and soon the friends who had so kindly welcomed him looked upon him as an evil spirit, and shrunk away as he approached.

At length his friend the dragon-fly besought him to leave the quiet home he had disturbed. Then Thistle was very angry, and while the dragon-fly was sleeping among the flowers that hung over the lake, he led an ugly spider to the spot, and bade him weave his nets about the sleeping insect, and bind him fast. The cruel spider gladly obeyed the ungrateful Fairy; and soon the poor fly could move neither leg nor wing. Then Thistle flew away through the wood, leaving sorrow and trouble behind him.

He had not journeyed far before he grew weary, and lay down to rest. Long he slept, and when he awoke, and tried to rise, his hand and wings were bound; while beside him stood two strange little figures, with dark faces and gar-

ments, that rustled like withered leaves ; who
cried to him, as he tried to get free,

"Lie still, you naughty Fairy, you are in the
Brownies' power, and shall be well punished for
your cruelty ere we let you go."

So poor Thistle lay sorrowfully, wondering
what would come of it, and wishing Lily-Bell
would come to help and comfort him ; but he had
left her, and she could not help him now.

Soon a troop of Brownies came rustling
through the air, and gathered round him, while
one wore an acorn-cup on his head, and was their
King, said, as he stood beside the trembling
Fairy,

"You have done many cruel things, and
caused much sorrow to happy hearts ; now you
are in my power, and I shall keep you prisoner
till you have repented. You cannot dwell on the
earth without harming the fair things given you
to enjoy, so you shall live alone in solitude and
darkness, till you have learned to find happiness
in gentle deeds, and forget yourself in giving joy
to others. When you have learned to do this, I
will set you free."

Then the Brownies bore him to a high, dark rock, and, entering a little door, led him to a small cell, dimly lighted by a crevice through which came a single gleam of sunlight; and there, through long, long days, poor Thistle sat alone, and gazed with wistful eyes at the little opening, longing to be out on the green earth. No one came to him but the silent Brownies who brought him his daily food; and with bitter tears he wept for Lily-Bell, mourning his cruelty and selfishness, seeking to do some kindly deed that might atone for his wrong doing.

A little vine that grew outside his prison rock

came creeping up, and looked in through the crevice, as if to cheer the lonely Fairy, who welcomed it most gladly, and daily sprinkled its soft leaves with his small share of water, that the little vine might live, even if it darkened more and more his dim cell.

The watchful Brownies saw this kind deed, and brought him fresh flowers, and many things, which Thistle gratefully received, though he never knew it was his kindness to the vine that gained for him these pleasures.

Thus did poor Thistle strive to be more gentle and unselfish, and grew daily happier and better.

Now while Thistledown was a captive in the lonely cell, Lily-Bell was seeking him far and wide, and sadly traced him by the sorrowing hearts he had left behind.

She healed the drooping flowers, cheered the Queen Bee's grief, and brought back her discontented subjects, restored the home to peace and order, and left them blessing her.

Thus she journeyed on, till she reached the forest where Thistledown had lost his freedom. She unbound the starving dragon-fly, and tended the wounded birds; but though all learned to love her, none could tell where the Brownies had borne her friend, till a little wind whispered by, and told her that a sweet voice had been heard, singing Fairy songs, deep in the moss-grown rock.

Thus Lily-Bell went seeking through the forests, listening for the voice. Long she looked and listened in vain, when one day, as she heard a faint low sound of music, and soon a distant voice mournfully singing,

RIGHT shines the summer sun,
 Soft is the summer air;
 Gayly the wood birds sing,
  Flowers are blooming.

"But in the dark, cold rock,
 Sadly I dwell,
Longing for thee, dear friend,
 Lily-Bell! Lily-Bell!"

"Thistle, dear Thistle, where
are you?" joyfully cried Lily-Bell,
as she flew from rock to rock.
But the voice was still, and she
would have looked in vain, had
she not seen a little vine, whose
green leaves fluttering to and fro
seemed beckoning her to come,
and as she stood among its
flowers she sang,

HROUGH sunlight
and summer air
I have sought for
thee long,
Guided by birds
and flowers,
And now by thy song.

"Thistledown! Thistledown!
O'er hill and dell
Hither to comfort thee
Comes Lily-Bell."

Then from the vine-leaves two little arms were stretched out to her, and Thistledown was found. So Lily-Bell made her home in the shadow of the vine, and brought such joy to Thistle, that his lonely cell seemed pleasanter to him than all the world beside, and he grew daily more like his gentle friend. But it did not last long, for one day she did not come. He watched and waited long, for the little face that used to peep smiling through the vine-leaves. He called and beckoned through the narrow opening, but no Lily-Bell answered, and he wept sadly as he thought of all she had done for him, and that now he could not go to seek and help her, for he had lost his freedom by his own cruel and wicked deeds.

At last he besought the silent Brownie earnestly to tell him whither she had gone.

"O let me go to her," prayed Thistle ; "if she is in sorrow I will comfort her, and show my gratitude for all she has done for me, dear Brownie, set me free, and when she is found I will come and be your prisoner again. I will bear and suffer any danger for her sake."

" Lily-Bell is safe," replied the Brownie ;

"come, you shall learn the trial that awaits you."

Then he led the wondering Fairy from his prison, to a group of tall, drooping ferns, beneath whose shade a large lily had been placed, forming a little tent, within which, on a couch of thick green moss, lay Lily-Bell in a deep sleep; the sunlight stole softly in, and all was cool and still.

"You cannot wake her," said the Brownie, as Thistle folded her arms tenderly about her. "It is a magic slumber, and she will not wake till you shall bring hither, gifts from the Earth, Air, and Water Spirits. 'Tis a long and weary task, for you have made no friends to help you, and will have to seek for them alone. This is a trial we shall give you; and if your love for Lily-Bell be strong enough to keep you from all cruelty and selfishness, and make you kind and loving as you should be, she will awake to welcome you, and love you still more fondly than before."

Then Thistle, with a last look on the little friend he loved so well, set forth alone to his long task.

The home of the Earth Spirits was the first to

find, and no one would tell him where to look. So far and wide he wandered, through gloomy forests and among lonely hills, with none to cheer him when sad and weary, none to guide him on his way.

On he went, thinking of Lily-Bell, and for her sake bearing all ; for in his quiet prison many gentle feelings and kindly thoughts had sprung up in his heart, and he now strove to be friends with all, and win for himself the love and confidence of those whom once he sought to harm and cruelly destroy.

But few believed him ; for they remembered his false promises and evil deeds, and would not trust him now ; so poor Thistle found few to love or care for him.

Long he wandered, and carefully he sought ; but could not find the Earth Spirits' home. And when at length he reached the pleasant garden where he and Lily-Bell first parted, he said within himself,

"Here I will stay awhile, and try to win by kindly deeds the flowers' forgiveness for the pain and sorrow I brought them long ago ; and they

may learn to love and trust me. So, even if ɪ
never find the Spirits, I shall be worthier Lily-
Bell's affection if I strive to atone for the wrong
I have done."

Then he went among the flowers, but they
closed their leaves, and shrank away, trembling
with fear; while the birds fled to hide among the
leaves as he passed.

This grieved poor Thistle, and he longed to
tell them how changed he had become; but they
would not listen. So he tried to show, by quiet
deeds of kindness, that he meant no harm to
them; and soon the kind-hearted birds pitied the
lonely Fairy, and when he came near sang cheering songs, and dropped ripe cherries in his path,
for he no longer broke their eggs or hurt their
little ones.

And when the flowers saw this, and found the
once cruel Elf now watering and tending little
buds, feeding hungry insects, and helping the
busy ants to bear their heavy loads, they shared
the pity of the birds, and longed to trust him;
but they dared not yet.

He came one day, while wandering through

the garden to the little rose he had harmed so
sadly. Many buds now bloomed beside her, and
her soft face glowed with motherly pride, as she
bent fondly over them. But when Thistle came
he saw with sorrow how she bade them close their
green curtains, and conceal themselves, for there
was danger near ; and, drooping still more closely
over them, she seemed to wait with trembling fear
the cruel Fairy's coming.

But no rude hands tore her little ones away,
no unkind words were spoken ; but a soft shower
of dew fell lightly upon them, and Thistle, bending tenderly over them said,

"Dear flower, forgive the sorrow I once
brought you, and trust me now for Lily-Bell's
sake. Her gentleness has changed my cruelty
to kindness, and I would gladly repay all for the
harm I have done; but none will love and trust
me now."

Then the little rose looked up, and while the
dew-drops shone like happy tears upon her leaves,
she said,

"I will love and trust you, Thistle, for you are
indeed much changed. Make your home among

us, and my sister flowers will soon learn to love
you as you deserve. Not for sweet Lily-Bell's
sake, but for your own, will I become your friend;
for you are kind and gentle now, and worthy of
our love. Look up, my little ones, there is no
danger near; look up, and welcome Thistle to
our home."

Then the little buds raised their rosy faces,
danced again upon their stems, and nodded kindly
at Thistle, who smiled on them through happy
tears, and kissed the sweet, forgiving rose, who
loved and trusted him when most forlorn and
friendless.

But the other flowers wondered among themselves, and Hyacinth said,

"If Rose-Leaf is his friend, surely we may be;
yet still I fear he may soon grow weary of his
gentleness, and be again the wicked Fairy he
once was, and we shall suffer for our kindness to
him now."

"Ah, do not doubt him!" cried warm-hearted
little Mignonette; "surely some good spirit has
changed the wicked Thistle into this good little
Elf. See how tenderly he lifts aside the leaves

that overshadow pale Harebell, and listen now how softly he sings as he rocks little Eglantine to sleep. He has done many friendly things, though none save Rose-Leaf has been kind to him, and he is very sad.

Last night when I awoke to draw my curtains closer, he sat weeping in the moonlight, so bitterly, I longed to speak a kindly word to him. Dear sisters, let us trust him."

And they all said little Mignonette was right; and, spreading wide their leaves, they bade him come, and drink their dew, and lie among the fragrant portals, striving to cheer his sorrow. Thistle told them all, and, after much whispering together, they said,

"Yes, we will help you to find the Earth Spirits, for you are striving to be good, and for love of Lily-Bell we will do much for you."

So they called a little bright-eyed mole, and said, "Downy-Back, we have given you a pleasant home among our roots, and you are a grateful little friend; so will you guide dear Thistle to the Earth Spirits' home?"

Downy-Back said, "Yes," and Thistle, thanking the kindly flowers, followed his little guide, through long, dark galleries, deeper and deeper into the ground; while the glow-worm flew before to light the way. On they went, and after a while reached a path lit up by bright jewels hung upon the walls. Here Downy-Back, and Glimmer, the glow-worm, left him, saying,

"We can lead you no farther; you must now go alone, and the music of the Spirits will guide you to their home."

Then they went quickly up the winding path, and Thistle guided by the sweet music went on alone.

He soon reached the lovely spot, whose golden halls were bright with jewels, which sparkled brightly, and threw many-colored shadows on the shining garments of the little Spirits, who danced below to the melody of soft, silvery bells.

Long Thistle stood watching the brilliant forms that flashed and sparkled round him; but he missed the flowers and the sunlight, and rejoiced that he was not an Earth Spirit.

At last they spied him out, and, gladly welcoming him, bade him join in their dance. But

Thistledown was too sad for that, and when he told them his story they no longer urged, but sought to comfort him ; and one whom they called little Sparkle (for her crown and robe shone with the brightest diamonds, said) : " You will have to work for us, ere you can win a gift to show the Brownies ; do you see those golden bells that make such music, as we wave them to and fro? We worked long and hard ere they were won, and you can win one of those, if you will do the task we give you."

And Thistle said, " No task will be too hard for me to do for dear Lily-Bell's sake."

Then they led him to a strange, dark place, lit up with torches ; where troops of Spirits flew busily to and fro, among damp rocks, and through dark galleries that led far down into the earth. " What do they here?" asked Thistle.

" I will tell you," replied Sparkle, " for I once worked here myself. Some of them watch above the flower-roots, and keep them fresh and strong ; others gather the clear drops that trickle from the damp rocks, and from a little spring, which, growing larger, rises to the light above, and gushes forth in some green field or lonely forest; where the wild-birds come to drink, and wood-flowers spread their thirsty leaves above the clear, cool waves, as they go dancing away, carrying joy and freshness wherever they go. Others shape the bright jewels into lovely forms, and make the good-luck pennies which we give to mortals whom we love. And here you must toil till the golden flower is won."

Then Thistle went among the Spirits, and joined in their tasks. He tended the flower-roots, gathered the water-drops, and formed the good-luck pennies. Long and hard he worked, and was often sad and weary, often tempted by unkind and selfish thoughts; but he thought of Lily-Bell, and strove to be kind and loving as she had been; and soon the Spirits learned to love the patient Fairy, who had left his home to toil among them for the sake of his gentle friend.

At length came little Sparkle to him, saying, "You have done enough; come now, and dance and feast with us, for the golden flower is won."

But Thistle could not stay, for half his task was not yet done; and he longed for sunlight and

Lily-Bell. So, taking a kind farewell, he hastened through the torch-lit path up to the light again; and, spreading his wings, flew over hill and dale till he reached the forest where Lily-Bell lay sleeping.

It was early morning, and the rosy light shone brightly through the lily-leaves upon her, as Thistle entered, and laid his first gift at the Brownie King's feet.

"You have done well," said he, "we hear good tidings of you from bird and flower, and you are truly seeking to repair the evil you have done. Take now one look at your little friend, and then go forth to seek from the Air Spirits your second gift."

Then Thistle said farewell again to Lily-Bell, and flew far and wide among the clouds, seeking the Air Spirits; but though he wandered till his weary wings could bear him no longer, it was in vain. So, faint and sad, he lay down to rest on a broad vine-leaf, that fluttered gently in the wind; and as he lay, he saw beneath him the home of the kind bees whom he had so disturbed, and Lily-Bell had helped and comforted

"I will seek to win their pardon, and show them that I am no longer the cruel Fairy who so harmed them," thought Thistle, "and when they become again my friends, I will ask their help to find the Air Spirits; and if I deserve it, they will gladly aid me on my way."

So he flew down into the field below, and hastened busily from flower to flower, till he had filled a tiny blue-bell with sweet, fresh honey. Then he stole softly to the hive, and, placing it near the door, concealed himself to watch. Soon his friend Nimble-Wing came flying home, and when he spied the little cup, he hummed with joy, and called his companions around him.

"Surely, some good Elf has placed it here for us," said they; "let us bear it to our Queen; it is so fresh and fragrant it will be a fit gift for her;" and they joyfully took it in, little dreaming who had placed it there.

So each day Thistle filled a flower-cup, and laid it at the door; and each day the bees wondered more and more, for many strange things happened. The field-flowers told of the good spirit who watched over them, and the birds sang

of the same kind little Elf bringing soft moss for
their nests, and food for their hungry ones ; while
all around the hive had grown fairer since the
Fairy came.

But the bees never saw him, for he feared he
had not yet done enough to win their forgiveness
and friendship ; so he lived alone among the
vines, daily bringing them honey, and doing
some kindly action.

At length, as he lay sleeping in a flower-bell,
a little bee came wandering by, and he knew him
for the wicked Thistle ; so he called his friends,
and, as they flew murmuring around him he
awoke.

"What shall we do to you, naughty Elf?"
said they. "You are in our power, and we will
sting you if you are not still."

"Let us close the flower-leaves around him
and leave him here to starve," cried one, who
had not forgotten all the sorrow Thistle had
caused them long ago.

"No, no, that were very cruel, dear Buzz,"
said little one ; "let us take him to our Queen,
and she will tell us how to show our anger for

wicked deeds he did. See how bitterly he weeps; be kind to him, he will not harm us more."

"You good little Hum!" cried a kind-hearted robin who hopped near to listen to the bees. "Dear friends, do you not know that this is the good little Fairy who has dwelt so quietly among us, watching over bird and blossom, giving joy to all he helps? It is he who brings the honey-cup each day to you, and then goes silently away, that you may never know who works so faithfully for you. Be kind to him, for if he has done wrong, he has repented of it, as you may see."

"Can this be naughty Thistle?" said Nimble-Wing.

"Yes, it is I," said Thistle, "but no longer cruel and unkind. I have tried to win your love by patient industry. Ah, trust me now, and you shall see I am not naughty Thistle any more."

Then the wondering bees led him to their Queen, and when he had told his tale, and begged their forgiveness, it was gladly given; and all strove to show him that he was loved and trusted. Then he asked if they could tell him where the Air Spirts dwelt, for he must not forget dear Lily-Bell; and to his great joy the Queen said, "Yes," and bade little Hum guide Thistle to Cloud Land.

Little Hum joyfully obeyed; and Thistle followed him, and as he flew higher and higher among the soft clouds, till in the distance they saw a radiant light.

"There is their home, and I must leave you now, dear Thistle," said the little bee; and bidding him farewell, he flew singing back, while Thistle, following the light, soon found himself in the Air Spirits' home.

The sky was gold and purple like an autumn sunset, and long walls of brilliant clouds lay round him. A rosy light shone through the silvery mist on gleaming columns and the rainbow roof; soft, fragrant winds whispered by; and airy little forms were flitting to and fro.

Long Thistle wondered at the beauty round him, and then he went among the shining Spirits, told his tale, and asked a gift.

But they answered like the Earth Spirits. "You must serve us first, and then we will gladly give you a robe of sunlight like our own?"

And then they told him how they wafted
flower seeds over the earth, to beautify and
brighten lonely spots ; how they watched over the
blossoms by day, and scattered dews at night,
brought sunlight into darkened places, and soft
winds to refresh and cheer.

"These are the things we do," said they,
" and you must aid us for a time."

And Thistle gladly went with the lovely Spirits ;
by day he joined the sunlight and breeze in their
silent work ; by night, with Star-Light and her
sister spirits, he flew over the moon-lit earth,
dropping cool dew upon the folded flowers, and
bringing happy dreams to sleeping mortals. Many
a kind deed was done, many a gentle word was
spoken, and each day lighter grew his heart, and
stronger his power of giving joys to others.

At length Star-light bade him work no more,
and gladly gave him the gift that he had won.
Then his second task was done, and he flew gayly
back to the green earth and slumbering Lily-Bell.

The silvery moonlight shone upon her, as he
came to give his second gift ; and the Brownie
spoke more kindly than before.

"One more trial, Thistle, and she will awake. Go bravely forth and win your last and hardest gift."

Then with a light heart Thistle journeyed away to the brooks and rivers, seeking the Water Spirits. But he looked in vain; till, wandering through the forest where the Brownie took him captive, he stopped beside the quiet lake.

As he stood here he heard a sound of pain, and, looking in at the tall grass at his side, he saw the dragon-fly whose kindness he once repaid by pain and sorrow, and who now lay suffering and alone.

Thistle bent tenderly beside him, saying, "Dear Flutter, do not fear me. I will gladly ease your pain, if you will let me; I am your friend, and long to show you how I grieve for all the wrong I did you, when you were so kind to me. Forgive, and let me help and comfort you."

Then he bound up the broken wing, and spoke so tenderly that Flutter doubted him no longer, and was his friend again.

Day by day did Thistle watch beside him, making little beds of cool, fresh moss for him to rest upon, fanning him while he slept, and singing sweet songs to cheer him when awake. And often when poor Flutter longed to be dancing once again over the blue waves, the Fairy bore him in his arms to the lake, and on a broad leaf, with a green flag for a sail, they floated on the still water; while the dragon-fly's companions flew about them, playing merry games.

At length the broken wing was well, and Thistle said he must again seek the Water Spirits. "I can tell you where to find them," said Flutter; "you must follow yonder little brook, and it will lead you to the sea, where the Spirits dwell. I would gladly do more for you, dear Thistle, but I cannot, for they live beneath the waves. You will find some kind friend to aid you on your way; and so farewell."

Thistle followed the little brook, as it flowed through field and valley, growing even larger, till it reached the sea. Here the wind blew freshly, and the great waves rolled and broke at Thistle's feet, as he stood upon the shore, watching the billows dancing and sparkling in the sun.

"How shall I find the Spirits in this great sea,

with none to help or guide me? Yet it is my last task, and for Lily-Bell's sake I must not fear or falter now," said Thistle. So he flew hither and thither over the sea, looking through the waves. Soon he saw, far below, the branches of the coral tree.

"They must be here," thought he, and, folding his wings, he plunged into the deep, cold sea. But he saw awful monsters and dark shapes that gathered round him; and, trembling with fear, he struggled up again.

The great waves tossed him to and fro, and cast him bruised and faint upon the shore. Here he lay weeping bitterly, till a voice beside him said, "Poor little Elf, what has befallen you? These rough waves are not fit playmates for so delicate a thing as you. Tell me your sorrow, and I will comfort you."

And Thistle, looking up, saw a white sea-bird at his side, who tried with friendly words to cheer him. So he told his wanderings, and how he sought the Sea Spirits.

"Surely, if bee and blossom do their part to help you, birds should aid you too," said the Sea-

bird. "I will call my friend, the Nautilus, and he
will bear you safely to the Coral Palace where the
Spirits dwell." So, spreading his great wings, he
flew away, and soon Thistle saw a little boat come
dancing over the waves, and wait beside the shore
for him.

In he sprang. Nautilus raised his little sail to
the wind, and the light boat glided swiftly over
the blue sea. At last Thistle cried, "I see lovely
arches far below; let me go, it is the Spirits'
home."

"Nay, close your eyes, and trust to me. I
will bear you safely down," said Nautilus.

So Thistle closed his eyes, and listened to the
murmur of the sea, as they sank slowly through
the waves. The soft sound lulled him to sleep,
and when he awoke the boat was gone, and he
stood among the Water Spirits, in their strange
and lovely home.

Lofty arches of snow-white coral bent above
him, and the walls of brightly tinted shells were
wreathed with lovely sea-flowers, and the sunlight shining on the waves cast silvery shadows
on the ground, where sparkling stones glowed

in the sand. A cool, fresh wind swept through
the waving garlands of bright sea-moss, and the
distant murmur of dashing waves came softly on
the air. Soon troops of graceful Spirits flittered
by, and when they found the wondering Elf, they
gathered round him, bringing pearl-shells heaped
with precious stones, and all rare, strange gifts that
lie beneath the sea. But Thistle wished for none
of these, and when his tale was told, the kindly
Spirits pitied him; and little Pearl sighed, as she
told him of the long and weary task he must perform, ere he could win a crown of snow-white
pearls like these they wore. But Thistle had
gained strength and courage in his wanderings,
and did not falter now, when they led him to a
place among the coral-workers, and told him he
must labor here, till the spreading branches
reached the light air, through the waves that
danced above.

With a patient hope that he might yet be
worthy of Lily-Bell, the Fairy left the lovely spirits
and their pleasant home, to toil among the coral-
builders, where all was strange and dim. Long,
long, he worked; but still the waves rolled far

above them, and his task was not yet done; and many bitter tears poor Thistle shed, and sadly he pined for air and sunlight, the voice of birds and breath of flowers. Often, folded in the magic garments which the Spirits gave him, that he might pass unharmed among the fearful creatures dwelling there, he rose to the surface of the sea, and, gliding through the waves, gazed longingly upon the hills, now looking blue and dim so far away, or watched the flocks of summer birds, journeying to a warmer land; and they brought sad memories of green old forests, and sunny fields, to the lonely little Fairy floating on the great, wild sea.

Day after day went by, and slowly Thistle's task drew towards an end. Busily toiled the coral-workers, but more busily toiled he; insect and Spirit daily wondered more and more, at the industry and patience of the silent little Elf, who had a friendly word for all, though he never joined them in their sport.

Higher and higher grew the coral-boughs, and lighter grew the Fairy's heart, while thoughts of dear Lily-Bell cheered him on, as day by day he

steadily toiled; and when at length the sun shone
on his work, and it was done, he stayed but to
take the garland he had won, and to thank the
good Spirits for their love and care. Then up
through the cold, blue waves he swiftly glided,
and, shaking the bright drops from his wings,
soared singing up to the sunny sky.

On through the fragrant air went Thistle, looking with glad face upon the fair, fresh earth below,
where flowers looked smiling up, and green trees
bowed their graceful heads as if to welcome him.
Soon the forest where Lily-Bell lay sleeping rose
before him, and as he passed along the cool
wood-paths, never had they seemed so fair.

But when he came where his little friend had
slept, it was no longer the dark silent spot where
he last saw her. Garlands hung from every tree,
and the fairest flowers filled the air with their
sweet breath. Birds' gay voices echoed far and
wide, and the little brook went singing by, beneath the arching ferns that bent above it; green
leaves rustled in the summer wind, and the air
was full of music. But the fairest sight was Lily-
Bell, as she lay on the couch of velvet moss that

Fairy hands had spread. The golden flower lay beside her, and the glittering robe was folded round her little form. The warmest sunlight fell upon her, and the softest breezes lifted her shining hair.

Happy tears fell fast, as Thistle folded his arms around her, crying, "O Lily-Bell, dear Lily-Bell, awake! I have been true to you, and now my task is done."

Then, with a smile, Lily-Bell awoke, and looked with wondering eyes upon the beauty that had risen round her.

"Dear Thistle, what mean these fair things, and why are we in this lovely place?"

"Listen, Lily-Bell," said the Brownie King, as he appeared beside her. And then he told her all that Thistle had done to show his love for her; how he had wandered far and wide to seek the Fairy gifts, and toiled long and hard to win them; how he had been loving, true, and tender, when most lonely and forsaken.

"Bird, bee, and blossom have forgiven him, and none is more loved and trusted now by all, than the once cruel Thistle," said the King, as he bent down to the happy Elf, who bowed low before him.

"You have learned the beauty of a gentle, kindly heart, dear Thistle; and you are now worthy to become the friend of her for whom you have done so much. Place the crown upon her head, for she is Queen of all the Forest Fairies now."

And as the crown showed on the head that Lily-Bell bent down on Thistle's breast, the forest seemed alive with little forms, who sprang from flower and leaf, and gathered round her, bringing gifts for their new Queen.

"If I am Queen, then you are King, dear Thistle," said the Fairy. "Take the crown, and I will have a wreath of flowers. You have toiled and suffered for my sake, and you alone should rule over these little Elves whose love you have won."

"Keep your crown, Lily-Bell, for yonder come the Spirits with their gifts to Thistle," said the Brownie. And, as he pointed with his wand, out from among the mossy roots of an old tree came trooping the Earth Spirits, their flower-bells ringing softly as they came, and their jewelled garments glittering in the sun. On to where Thistledown stood beneath the shadows of the flowers, with Lily-Bell beside him, went· the Spirits; and then forth sprang little Sparkle, waving a golden flower, whose silvery music filled the air. "Dear Thistle," said the shining Spirit, "what you toiled so faithfully to win for another, let us offer now as a token of our love for you."

As she ceased, down through the air came floating bands of lovely Spirits, bringing a shining robe, and they too told their love for the gentle Fairy who had dwelt with them.

Then softly on the breeze came distant music, growing ever nearer, till over the rippling waves came the singing Water Spirits, in their boats of many-colored shells; and as they placed their glittering crown on Thistle's head, loud rang the flowers, and joyously sang the birds, while all the Forest Fairies cried, with silvery voices, "Lily-Bell and Thistledown! Long live our King and Queen!"

"Have you a tale for us too, dear Violet-Eyes?" said the Queen as Zephyr ceased. The

little Elf thus named looked from among the
Flower-leaves where she sat, and with a smile
replied, " As I was weaving garlands in the field,
I heard a primrose tell this tale to her friend
Golden-ROD."

Little Bud.

In a great forest, high
up among the green boughs, lived
Bird Brown-Breast, and his bright-
eyed little mate. They were now
very happy; their home was done,
the four blue eggs lay in the soft
nest, and the little wife sat still and
patient on them, while the husband
sang, and told her charming tales,
and brought her sweet berries and
little worms.

Things went smoothly on, till one day she found in the nest a little white egg, with a golden band about it.

"My friend," cried she, "come and see! Where can this fine egg have come from? My four are here, and this also; what think you of it?"

The husband shook his head gravely, and said, "Be not alarmed, my love; it is doubtless some good Fairy who has given us this, and we shall find some gift within; do not let us touch it, but do you sit carefully upon it, and we shall see in time what has been sent us."

So they said nothing about it, and soon they had four little chirping children; and then the white egg opened, and, behold, a little maiden lay singing within. Then how amazed were they, and how they welcomed her, as she lay warm beneath the mother's wing, and how the young birds did love her.

Great joy was in the forest, and proud were the parents of their family, and still more of the little one who had come to them; while all the neighbors flocked in, to see Dame Brown-Breast's

Flower Fables—9

little child. And the tiny maiden talked to them,
and sang so merrily, that they could have listened
for ever. Soon she was the joy of the whole
forest, dancing from tree to tree, making every
nest her home, and none were ever so welcome
as little Bud; and so they lived right merrily in
the green old forest.

The father now had much to do to supply his
family with food, and choice morsels did he bring
little Bud. The wild fruits were her food, the
fresh dew in the flower-cups her drink; while the
green leaves served her for little robes; and thus
she found garments in the flowers of the field,
and a happy home with Mother Brown-Breast; and
all in the wood, from the stately trees to the little
mosses in the turf, were friends to the merry child.

And each day she taught the young birds sweet
songs, and as their gay music ran through the old
forest, the stern, dark pines ceased their solemn
waving, that they might hear the soft sounds
stealing through the dim-wood paths, and mortal
children came to listen, saying softly, "Hear the
flowers sing, and touch them not, for the Fairies
are here."

Then came a band of sad little Elves to Bud,
praying that they might hear the sweet music, and
when she took them by the hand, and spoke gently
to them, they wept and said sadly, when she asked
them whence they came,—

"We dwelt once in Fairy Land, and O how
happy we were then! But alas! we were not
worthy of so fair a home, and were sent forth into
the cold world. Look at our robes, they are like
the withered leaves; our wings are dim, our
crowns are gone, and we lead sad, lonely lives in
this dark forest. Let us stay with you; your gay
music sounds like Fairy songs, and you have such
a friendly way with you, and speak so gently to us.
It is good to be near one so lovely and so kind; and
you can tell us how we may again become fair and
innocent. Say we may stay with you, kind little
maiden."

And Bud said, "Yes," and they stayed; but
her kind little heart was grieved that they wept
so sadly, and all she could say could not make
them happy; till at last she said,—

"Do not weep, and I will go to Queen Dew-
Drop, and beseech her to let you come back. I

will tell her that you are repentant, and will do anything to gain her love again ; that you are sad,
and long to be forgiven. This will I say, and
more, and trust she will grant my prayer."

"She will not say no to you, dear Bud," said
the poor little Fairies ; "she will love you as we
do, and if we can but come again to our lost
home, we cannot give you thanks enough. Go,
Bud, and if there be power in Fairy gifts, you
shall be as happy as our hearts' love can make
you."

The tidings of Bud's departure flew through
the forest, and all her friends came to say farewell, as with the morning sun she would go ; and
each brought some little gift, for the land of
Fairies was far way, and she must journey long.

"Nay, you shall not go on your feet, my
child," said Mother Brown-Breast ; "your friend
Golden-Wing shall carry you. Call him hither,
that I may seat you rightly, for if you should fall
off, my heart would break."

Then up came Golden-Wing, and Bud was
safely seated on the cushion of violet leaves ; and
it was really charming to see her merry little face

peeping from under the broad brim of her cowslip hat, as her butterfly steed stood waving his
bright wings in the sunlight. Then came the bee
with his yellow honey-bags, which he begged she
would take, and a little brown spider that lived
under the great leaves brought a veil for her hat,
and besought her to wear it, lest the sun should
shine too brightly ; while the ant came bringing a
tiny strawberry, lest she should miss her favorite
fruit. The mother gave her good advice, and the
papa stood with his head on one side, and his
round eyes twinkling with delight, to think that
his little Bud was going to Fairy Land.

Then they all sang gayly together, till she
passed out of sight over the hills, and they saw
her no more.

And now Bud left the old forest far behind
her. Golden-Wing bore her swiftly along, and
she looked down on the green mountains and the
peasants' cottages, that stood among over-shadow-
ing trees ; and the earth looked bright, with its
broad, blue rivers winding through soft meadows,
the singing of birds, and flowers, who kept their
bright eyes ever on the sky.

And she sang gayly as they floated in the clear air, while her friend kept time with his waving wings, and ever as they went along all grew fairer; and thus they came to Fairy Land.

As Bud passed through the gates, she no longer wondered that the exiled Fairies wept and sorrowed for the lovely home they had lost. Bright clouds floated in the sunny sky, casting a rainbow light on the Fairy palaces below, where the Elves were dancing; while the low, sweet voices of the singing flowers sounded softly through the fragrant air, and mingled with the music of the rippling waves, as they flowed on beneath the blossoming vines that drooped above them.

All was bright and beautiful; but kind little Bud would not linger, for the forms of the weeping Fairies were before her, and though the blossoms nodded gayly on their stems to welcome her, and the soft winds kissed her cheek, she would not stay, but on to the Flower Palace she went, into a pleasant hall whose walls were formed of crimson roses, amid whose leaves sat little Elves, making sweet music on their harps.

LITTLE BUD STARTS FOR FAIRYLAND.

When they saw Bud, they gathered round her, and led her through the flower-wreathed arches to a group of the most beautiful Fairies, who were gathered about a stately lily, in whose fragrant cup sat one whose purple robe and glittering crown told she was their Queen.

Bud knelt before her, and, while tears streamed down her little face, she told her errand, and pleaded earnestly that the exiled Fairies might be forgiven, and not be left to pine far from their friends and kindred. And as she prayed, many wept with her, and when she ceased, and waited for her answer, many knelt beside her, praying forgiveness for the unhappy Elves.

With tearful eyes, Queen Dew-Drop replied, "Little Maiden, your prayer has softened my heart. They shall not be left sorrowing and alone, nor shall you go back without a kindly word to cheer and comfort them. We shall pardon their fault, and when they can bring hither a perfect Fairy crown, robe and wand, they shall again be received as children of their loving Queen. The task is hard, for none but the best and purest can form the Fairy garments ; yet with patience they may yet restore their robes to their former brightness. Farewell, good little maiden; come with them, for but you they would have dwelt forever without the walls of Fairy Land."

"Good speed to you, and farewell," cried they all, as, with loving messages to their poor friends, they bore her to the gates.

Day after day toiled little Bud, cheering the Fairies, who, angry and disappointed, would not listen to her gentle words, but turned away and sat alone weeping. They grieved her kind heart with many cruel words; but patiently she bore them, and when they told her they could never perform so hard a task, and must dwell forever in the dark forest, she answered gently, that the snow-white lily must be planted, and watered with repentant tears, before the robe of innocence could be worn; that the sun of love must shine in their hearts, before the light could return to their dim crowns, and deeds of kindness must be performed, ere the power would come again to their now useless wands.

Then they planted the lilies; but they soon drooped and died, and no light came to their

crowns. They did no gentle deeds, but cared
only for themselves; and when they found their
labor was in vain, they tried no longer, but sat
weeping. Bud, with ceaseless toil and patient
care, tended the lilies, which bloomed brightly, the
crowns grew bright, and in her hands the wands
had power over birds and blossoms, forgetful of
herself. And the idle Fairies, with thankful
words, took the garments from her, and then Bud
went forth to Fairy Land, and stood with beating
hearts before the gates, where crowds of Fairy
friends came forth to welcome them.

But when Queen Dew-Drop touched them
with her wand, as they passed in, the light faded
from their crowns, their robes became like withered leaves, and the wands were powerless.

Amid the tears of all the Fairies, the Queen
led them to the gates, and said,

"Farewell! It is not in my power to aid you;
innocence and love are not within your hearts,
and were it not for this untiring little maiden,
who has toiled while you have wept, you would
never have entered your lost home. Go and

strive again, for till all is once more fair and pure,. I cannot call you mine."

"Farewell !" sang the weeping Fairies, as the gates closed on their outcast friends, who, humbled and broken hearted, gathered around Bud; and she, with cheering words, guided them back to the forest.

Time passed on, and the Fairies had done nothing to gain their lovely home again. They wept no longer, but watched little Bud, as she daily tended the flowers, restoring their strength and beauty, or with gentle words flew from nest to nest, teaching the little birds to live happily together; and wherever she went blessings fell, and loving hearts filled with gratitude.

Then, one by one, the Elves secretly did some little work of kindness, and found a quiet joy come back to repay them. Flowers looked lovingly up as they passed, birds sang to cheer them when sad thoughts made them weep. And soon little Bud found out their gentle deeds, and her friendly words gave them new strength. So day after day they followed her, and like a band of guardian spirits they flew far and wide, carrying with them joy and peace.

And not only the birds and flowers blessed
them, but human beings also ; for with tender
hands they guided little children from danger, and
kept their young hearts free from evil thoughts ;
they whispered soothing words to the sick, and
brought sweet odors and fair flowers to their
lonely rooms.   They sent lovely visions to the old
and blind, to make their hearts young and bright
with happy thoughts.

But most tenderly did they watch over the
poor and sorrowing, and many a poor mother
blessed the unseen hands that laid food before
her hungry little ones, and folded warm garments
around their naked limbs.   Many a poor man
wondered at the fair flowers that sprang up in his
little garden-plot, cheering him with their bright
forms, and making his dreary home fair with
loveliness, and looked at his once barren field,
where now waved the golden corn, turning its
broad leaves to the warm sun, and promising a
store of golden ears to give him food ; while the
care-worn face grew bright and the troubled heart
filled with gratitude towards the invisible spirits
who had brought him such joy.

Thus time passed on, and though the exiled Fairies longed often for their home, still, knowing they did not deserve it, they toiled on, hoping one day to see the friends they had lost; while the joy of their own hearts made their life full of happiness.

One day came little Bud to them saying:

"Listen, dear friends. I have a hard task to offer you. It is a great sacrifice for you light-loving Fairies to dwell through the long winter in the dark, cold earth, watching over flower-roots, to keep them free from the little grubs and worms that seek to harm them. But in the sunny Spring when they bloom again, their love and gratitude will give you happy homes among their bright leaves.

" It is a wearisome task, and I can give you no reward for all your tender care, but the blessings of the gentle flowers you have saved from death. Gladly would I aid you; but my winged friends are preparing for their journey to warmer islands, and I must teach their little ones to fly, and see them safely on their way. Then, through the winter must I seek the dwellings of the poor and suffering, comfort the sick and lonely, and give hope and courage to those who in poverty are led astray. These things must I do; but when the flowers bloom again I will be with you, to welcome back our friends from over the sea."

Then with tears, the Fairies answered, "Ah, good little Bud, you have taken the hardest task yourself, and who will repay you for all your deeds of tenderness and mercy in the great world? Should evil befall you, our hearts would break. We will labor trustingly in the earth, and thoughts of you shall cheer us; for without you we had been worthless beings, and never known the joy that kindly actions bring. Yes, dear Bud, we will gladly toil among the roots, that the fair flowers may wear their gayest robes to welcome you.

Then deep in the earth the Fairies dwelt, and no frost or snow could harm the blossoms they tended. Every little seed was laid in the soft earth, watered, and watched. Tender roots were folded in withered leaves, that no chilling drops might reach them; and safely dreamed the flowers, till summer winds should call them forth;

while lighter grew each Fairy heart, as every
gentle deed was tenderly performed.

At length the snow was gone, and they heard
little voices calling them to come up ; but patiently they worked, till seed and root were green
and strong. Then, with eager feet, they hastened
to the earth above, where, over hill and valley,
bright flowers and budding trees smiled in the
warm sunlight, blossoms bent lovingly before
them, and rang their colored bells, till the fragrant air was full of music ; while the stately trees
waved their great arms above them, and scattered
soft leaves at their feet.

Then came the merry birds, making this wood
alive with gay voices, calling to one another, as
they flew among the vines, building their little
homes. Long waited the Elves, and at last she
came with Father Brown-Breast.

Happy days passed ; and summer flowers
were in their fullest beauty, when Bud bade the
Fairies come with her.

Mounted on bright-winged butterflies, they
flew over forest and meadow, till with joyful eyes
they saw the flower-crowned walls of Fairy Land.

Before the gates they stood, and soon troops of loving Elves came forth to meet them. And on through the sunny gardens they went, into the lily Hall, where, among the golden stamens of a graceful flower, sat the Queen; while on the broad, green leaves around it stood the bright-eyed little maids of honor.

Then, amid the deep silence, little Bud, leading the Fairies to the throne, said,

"Dear Queen, I here bring back your subjects, wiser for their sorrow, better for their hard trial; and now might any Queen be proud of them, and bow to learn from them that giving joy and peace to others brings it fourfold to us, bearing a double happiness in the blessings to those we help. Through the dreary months, when they might have dwelt among fair southern flowers, beneath a smiling sky, they toiled in the dark and silent earth, filling the hearts of the gentle Flower Spirits with grateful love, seeking no reward but the knowledge of their own good deeds, and the joy they always bring. This they have done unmurmuringly and alone; and now, far and wide, flower blessings fall upon them, and the summer winds bear the glad tidings unto those who droop in sorrow, and new joy and strength it brings, as they look lovingly for the friends whose gentle care hath brought happiness to their fair kindred.

"Are they not worthy of your love, dear Queen? Have they not won their lovely home? Say they are pardoned, and you have gained the love of their hearts pure as the snow-white robes now folded over them."

As bud ceased, she touched the wondering Fairies with her wand, and the dark faded garments fell away; and beneath, the robes of lily-leaves glittered pure and spotless in the sunlight. Then, while happy tears fell, Queen Dew-Drop placed the bright crowns on the bowed heads of the kneeling Fairies, and laid before them the wands their own good deeds had rendered powerful.

They turned to thank little Bud for all her patient love, but she was gone; and high above, in the clear air, they saw the little form journeying back to the quiet forest.

She needed no reward but the joy she had given. The Fairy hearts were pure again, and her work was done; yet all Fairy Land had learned a lesson from gentle little Bud.

"Now, little Sunbeam, what have you to tell us?" said the Queen, looking down on a bright-eyed Elf, who sat half hidden in the deep moss at her feet.

"I too, like Star-Twinkle, have nothing but a song to offer," replied the Fairy; and then while the nightingale's sweet voice mingled with her own, she sang,

Clover-Blossom.

IN the quiet, pleasant meadow,
    Beneath a summer sky,
Where green old trees **their**
    branches waved,
    And winds went singing by;
Where a little brook went rippling
    So musically low,
And passing clouds cast shadows
    On the waving grass below;

Where low, sweet notes of brooding birds
　　Stole out on the fragrant air,
And golden sunlight shone undimmed
　　On all most fresh and fair ;
There bloomed a lovely sisterhood
　　Of happy little flowers,
Together in this pleasant home,
Through quiet summer hours.

No rude hand came to gather them,
　　No chilling winds to blight ;
Warm sunbeams smiled on them by day,
　　And soft dews fell at night.
So here, along the brook-side,
　　Beneath the green old trees,
The flowers dwelt among their friends,
　　The sunbeams and the breeze.

NE morning, as the flowers awoke,
  Fragrant, and fresh, and fair,
A little worm came creeping by,
  And begged a shelter there.
"Ah! pity and love me," sighed the worm,
  "I am lonely, poor, and weak;
A little spot for a resting-place,
  Dear flowers, is all I seek.
I am not fair, and have dwelt unloved
  By butterfly, bird, and bee.
They little knew that in this dark form
  Lay the beauty they may yet see.
Then let me lie in the deep green moss,
  And weave my little tomb,
And sleep my long, unbroken sleep
  'Till Spring's first flowers come.
Then will I come in fairer dress,
  And your gentle care repay
By the grateful love of the humble **worm;**
  Kind flowers, O let me stay!"

But the wild rose showed her little thorns,

   While her soft face glowed with pride;

The violet hid beneath the drooping ferns,

   And the daisy turned aside.

Little Houstonia scornfully laughed,

   As she danced on her slender stem;

While the cowslip bent to the rippling waves,

   And whispered the tale to them.

A blue-eyed grass looked down on the worm,

   As it silently turned away,

And cried, "Thou wilt harm our delicate leaves,

   And therefore thou canst not stay."

Then a sweet, soft voice called out from far,

   "Come hither, poor worm, to me;

The sun lies warm in this quiet spot,

   And I'll share my home with thee."

The wondering flowers looked up to see

   Who had offered the worm a home;

WAS a clover-blossom, whose flut-
tering leaves
   Seemed beckoning him to come;
It dwelt in a sunny little nook,
   Where cool winds rustled by,
And murmuring bees and butterflies came,
  On the flower's breast to lie.
Down through the leaves the sunlight stole,
  And seemed to linger there,
As if it loved to brighten the home
  Of one so sweet and fair.
Its rosy face smiled kindly down,
  As the friendless worm drew near;
And its low voice, softly whispering said,
  "Poor thing, thou art welcome here;
Close at my side, in the soft green moss,
  Thou wilt find a quiet bed,
Where thou canst softly sleep till Spring,
  With my leaves above thee spread.

I pity and love thee, friendless worm,
　　Though thou art not graceful or fair;
For many a dark unlovely form,
　　Hath a kind heart dwelling there;
No more o'er the green and pleasant earth,
　　Lonely and poor, shalt thou roam,
For a loving friend hast thou found in me,
　　And rest in my little home."
Then, deep in its quiet mossy bed,
　　Sheltered from sun and shower,
The grateful worm spun its winter tomb,
　　In the shadow of the flower.
And Clover guarded well its rest,
　　Till Autumn's leaves were sere,
Till all her sister flowers were gone,
　　And her winter sleep drew near.
Then her withered leaves were softly spread
　　O'er the sleeping worm below,
Ere the faithful little flower lay
　　Beneath the winter snow.

PRING came again, and the flowers
rose
From their quiet winter graves,
And gayly danced on their slender
stems,
And sang with the rippling waves.
Softly the warm winds kissed their cheeks ;
Brightly the sunbeams fell,
As, one by one, they came again
In their summer homes to dwell.
And little Clover bloomed once more,
Rosy, and sweet, and fair,
And patiently watched by the mossy bed,
For the worm still slumbered there.
Then her sister flowers scornfully cried,
As they waved in the summer air,
" The ugly worm was friendless and poor ;
Little Clover, why shouldst thou care?
Then watch no more, nor dwell alone,
Away from thy sister flowers ;

Come, dance and feast, and spend with us
  These pleasant summer hours.
We pity thee, foolish little flower,
  To trust what the false worm said;
He will not come in fairer dress,
  For he lies in the green moss dead."
But little Clover still watched on,
  Alone in her sunny home;
She did not doubt the poor worm's truth,
  And trusted he would come.

At last the small cell opened wide,
  And a glittering butterfly,
From out the moss, on golden wings,
  Soared up to the sunny sky.
Then the flowers cried aloud,
  " Clover, thy watch was in vain;
He only sought a shelter here,
  And never will come again."

ND the unkind flowers danced for
      joy,
   When they saw him thus depart;
For the love of a beautiful butterfly
   Is dear to a flower's heart.
   They feared he would stay in
      Clover's home,
And her tender care repay ;
So they danced for joy, when at last he rose
   And silently flew away.
Then little Clover bowed her head,
   While her soft tears fell like dew ;
For her gentle heart was grieved, to find
   That her sisters' word was true,
And the insect she had watched so long
   When helpless, poor, and lone,
Thankless for all her faithful care,
   On his golden wings had flown.
But as she drooped, in silent grief,
   She heard little Daisy cry,
"O sisters, look ! I see him now,
   Afar in the sunny sky ;

He is floating black from Cloud Land now,
    Borne by the fragrant air
Spread wide your leaves, that he may choose,
    The flower he deems most fair."
Then the Wild Rose glowed with a deeper blush,
    As she proudly waved on her stem ;
The Cowslip bent to the clear blue waves,
    And made her mirror of them.
Little Houstonia merrily danced,
    And spread her white leaves wide ;
While Daisy whispered her joy and hope,
    As she stood by her gay friends' side.
Violet peeped from the tall green ferns,
    And lifted her soft blue eye
To watch the glittering form, that shone
    Afar in the summer sky.
They thought no more of the ugly worm,
    Who once had wakened their scorn ;
But looked and longed for the butterfly now,
    As the soft wind bore him on.

EARER and nearer the bright
form came,
And fairer the blossoms grew;
Each welcomed him, in her sweet-
est tones;
Each offered her honey and dew.
But in vain did they beckon, and smile, and call,
And wider their leaves unclose;
The glittering form still floated on,
By Violet, Daisy, and Rose.
Lightly it flew to the pleasant home
Of the flower most truly fair,
On Clover's breast he softly lit,
And folded his bright wings there.
" Dear flower," the Butterfly whispered low,
"Long hast thou waited for me;
Now I am come, and my grateful love
Shall brighten thy home for thee;
Thou hast loved and cared for me, when alone,
Hast watched o'er me long and well;

And now will I strive to show the thanks
    The poor worm could not tell.
Sunbeam and breeze shall come to thee,
    And the coolest dews that fall ;
Whate'er a flower can wish is thine,
    For thou art worthy all.
And the home thou shared with the friendless
    worm
    The butterfly's home shall be;
And thou shalt find, dear, faithful flower,
    A loving friend in me."
Then through the long, bright summer hours
    Through sunshine and through shower,
Together in their happy home
    Dwelt butterfly and flower.

"Ah, that is very lovely," cried the Elves,
gathering round little Sunbeam as she ceased, to
place a garland in her hair and praise her song.

"Now," said the Queen, "call hither Moonlight
and Summer Wind, for they have seen many

pleasant things in their long wanderings, and will gladly tell us them."

"Most joyfully will we do our best, dear Queen," said the Elves, as they folded their wings beside her.

"Now, Summer-Wind," said Moonlight, "till your turn comes, do you sit here and fan me while I tell this tale of

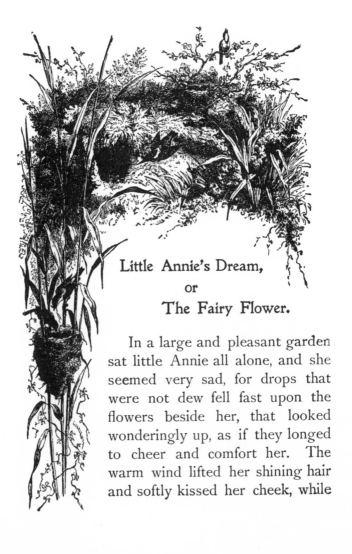

Little Annie's Dream,
or
The Fairy Flower.

In a large and pleasant garden sat little Annie all alone, and she seemed very sad, for drops that were not dew fell fast upon the flowers beside her, that looked wonderingly up, as if they longed to cheer and comfort her. The warm wind lifted her shining hair and softly kissed her cheek, while the sunbeams, looking most kindly in her face, made little rainbows in her tears, and lingered lovingly about her. But Annie paid no heed to sun, or wind, or flower; still the bright tears fell, and she forgot all but sorrow.

"Little Annie, tell me why you weep," said a low voice in her ear; and, looking up, the child beheld a little figure standing on a vine-leaf at her side; a lovely face smiled on her, from amid bright locks of hair, and shining wings were folded on a white and glittering robe, that fluttered in the wind.

"Who are you, lovely thing?" cried Annie, smiling through her tears.

"I am a Fairy, little child, and am come to help and comfort you; now tell me why you weep, and let me be your friend," replied the spirit, as she smiled more kindly on Annie's wondering face.

"And are you really, a little Elf, such as I read of in my fairy books? Do you ride on butterflies, sleep in flower-cups, and live among the clouds?"

"Yes, all these things I do, and many stranger still, that all your fairy books can never tell; but now, dear Annie," said the Fairy, bending nearer, "tell me why I found no sunshine on your face; why are these great drops shining in the flowers, and why do you sit alone when bird and bee are calling you to play?"

"Ah, you will not love me any more if I should tell you all," said Annie, while the tears began to fall again; "I am not happy, for I am not good; how shall I learn to be a patient, gentle child? Good little Fairy, will you teach me?"

"Gladly will I aid you, Annie, and if you truly wish to be a happy child, you must learn to conquer many passions that you cherish now, and make your heart a home for the gentle feelings and happy thoughts; the task is hard, but I will give this fairy flower to help and counsel you. Bend hither, that I may place it in your breast; no hand can take it hence, till I unsay the spell that holds it there."

And as thus she spoke, the Elf took from her bosom a graceful flower, whose snow-white leaves shone with a strange light. "This is a fairy flower," said the Elf, "invisible to every eye save yours; now listen while I tell its power,

Annie. When your heart is filled with loving thoughts, when some kindly deed has been done, some duty well performed, then from the flower there will arise the sweetest, softest fragrance, to reward and gladden you. But when an unkind word is on your lips, when a selfish, angry feeling rises in your heart, or an unkind, cruel deed is to be done, then will you hear the soft, low chime of the flower-bell; listen to its warning, let the word remain unspoken, the deed undone, and in the quiet joy of your own heart, and the magic perfume of your bosom flower, you will find a sweet reward."

"O kind and generous Fairy, how can I ever thank you for this lovely gift?" cried Annie. "I will be true, and listen to my little bell whenever it may ring. But shall I never see you more? Ah! if you would only stay with me, I should indeed be good."

"I cannot stay now, little Annie," said the Elf, "but when another Spring comes round, I shall be here again, to see how well the fairy gift has done its work. And now farewell, dear child; be faithful to yourself, and the magic flower will never fade."

Then the gentle Fairy folded her little arms around Annie's neck, laid a soft kiss on her cheek, and, spreading her shining wings, flew singing up among the white clouds floating in the sky.

And little Annie sat among her flowers, and watched with wondering joy the fairy blossoms shining on her breast.

The pleasant days of Spring and Summer passed away, and in little Annie's garden Autumn flowers were blooming everywhere, with each day's sun and dew growing still more beautiful and bright ; but the fairy flower, that should have been the loveliest of all, hung pale and drooping on little Annie's bosom ; its fragrance seemed quite gone, and the clear, low music of its warning chime rang often in her ear.

When first the Fairy placed it there, she had been pleased with her new gift, and for a while obeyed the fairy bell, and often tried to win some fragrance from the flower, by kind and pleasant words and actions ; then, as the Fairy said, she found a sweet reward in the strange, soft perfume of the magic blossom, as it shone upon her breast; but selfish thoughts would come to tempt her, she would yield, and unkind words fell from her lips, and then the flower drooped pale and scentless, the fairy bell rang mournfully, Annie would forget her better resolutions, and be again a selfish, wilful little child.

At last she tried no longer, but grew angry with the faithful flower, and would have torn it from her breast; but the fairy spell still held it fast, and all her angry words but made it ring a louder, sadder peal. Then she paid no heed to the silvery music sounding in her ear, and each day grew still more unhappy, discontented and unkind; so, when the Autumn days came round, she was no better for the gentle Fairy's gift, and longed for Spring, that it might be returned; for now the constant echo of the mournful music made her very sad.

One sunny morning, when the fresh, cool winds were blowing, and not a cloud was in the sky, little Annie walked among her flowers, looking carefully into each, hoping thus to find the Fairy, who alone could take the magic blossom

from her breast. But she lifted up their drooping leaves, peeped into their dewy cups in vain ;
no little Elf lay hidden there, and she turned
sadly from them all, saying, " I will go out into
the fields and woods, and seek her there. I
will not listen to this tiresome music more, nor
wear this withered flower longer." So out into
the fields she went, where the long grass rustled
as she passed, and timid birds looked at her from
their nests ; where lovely wild-flowers nodded in
the wind, and opened wide their fragrant leaves,
to welcome in the murmuring bees, while butterflies, like winged flowers, danced and glittered in
the sun.

Little Annie looked, searched, and asked them
all if anyone could tell her of the Fairy whom
she sought ; but the birds looked wonderingly at
her with their soft, bright eyes, and still sang
on ; the flowers nodded wisely on their stems,
but did not speak, while butterfly and bee buzzed
and fluttered away, one far too busy, the other
too idle, to stay and tell her what she asked.

Then she went through broad fields of yellow
grain, that waved around her like a golden forest ;

here crickets chirped, grasshoppers leaped, and busy ants worked, but they could not tell her what she longed to know.

"Now I will go among the hills," said Annie, "she may be there." So up and down the green hillsides went her little feet ; long she searched and vainly she called ; but still no Fairy came. Then by the riverside she went, and asked the gay dragon-flies and the cool, white lilies, if the Fairy had been there ; but the blue waves rippled on the white sand at her feet, and no voice answered her.

Then into the forest little Annie went, and as she passed along the dim, cool paths, the wood-flowers smiled up in her face, gay squirrels peeped at her, as they swung amid the vines, and doves cooed softly as she wandered by, but none could answer her. So weary with her long and useless search, she sat amid the ferns, and feasted on the rosy strawberries that grew beside her, watching meanwhile the crimson evening clouds that glowed around the setting sun.

The night wind rustled through the boughs, rocking the flowers to sleep ; the wild-birds sang

their evening hymns, and all within the wood
grew calm and still; paler and paler grew the
purple light, and lower and lower drooped little
Annie's head, the tall ferns bent to shield her
from the dew, the whispering pines sang a soft
lullaby, and when the Autumn moon rose up, her
silver light shone on the child, where pillowed on
green moss, she lay asleep amid the wood-flowers
in the dim old forest.

And all night long beside her stood the Fairy
she had sought, and by elfin spell and charm sent
to the little child this dream.

Little Annie dreamed she sat in her own garden, as she had often sat before, with angry feelings in her heart, and unkind words upon her lips.
The magic flower was ringing its soft warning, but
she paid no heed to anything, save her own
troubled thoughts; thus she sat, when suddenly a
low voice whispered in her ear,—

"Little Annie, look and see the evil things that
you are cherishing; I will clothe in fitting shapes
the thoughts and feelings that now dwell within
your heart, and you shall see how great their
power becomes, unless you banish them forever."

Then Annie saw, with fear and wonder, that the angry words she uttered changed to dark, unlovely forms, each showing plainly from what fault or passion it had sprung. Some of the shapes had scowling faces and bright, fiery eyes ; these were the spirits of Anger. Others with sullen, anxious looks, seemed gathering up all they could reach, and Annie saw that the more they gained, the less they seemed to have ; and these she knew were shapes of Selfishness. Spirits of Pride were there, who folded their shadowy garments round them, and turned scornfully from all the rest. These and many others little Annie saw, which had come from her own heart, and taken form before her eyes.

When first she saw them, they were small and weak ; but as she looked they seemed to grow and gather strength, and each gained a strange power over her. She could not drive them from her sight, and they grew ever stronger, darker, and more unlovely to her eyes. They seemed to cast black shadows over all around her, to dim the sunshine, blight the flowers, and drive away all bright and lovely things ; while rising slowly

round her Annie saw a high, dark wall, that
seemed to shut everything she loved; she dared
not move, or speak, but, with a strange fear at
her heart, sat watching the dim shapes that hov-
ered round her.

Higher and higher rose the shadowy wall,
slowly the flowers near her died, lingeringly the
sunlight faded; but at last they both were gone,
and left her all alone behind the gloomy wall.
Then the spirits gathered round her, whispering
strange things in her ear, bidding her obey, for
by her own will she had yielded up her heart to
be their home, and she was now their slave. Then
she could hear no more, but, sinking down among
the withered flowers, wept sad and bitter tears,
for her lost liberty and joy; then through the
gloom there shone a faint, soft light, and on her
breast she saw her fairy flower, upon whose snow-
white leaves her tears lay shining.

Clearer and brighter grew the radiant light, till
the evil spirits turned away to the dark shadow
of the wall, and left the child alone.

The light and perfume of the flower seemed
to bring new strength to Annie, and she rose up,

saying, as she bent to kiss the blossom on her breast, "dear flower, help and guide me now, and I will listen to your voice, and cheerfully obey my faithful fairy bell."

Then in her dream she felt how hard the spirit tried to tempt and trouble her, and how, but for her flower, they would have led her back, and made all dark and dreary as before. Long and hard she struggled, and tears often fell ; but after each new trial brighter shone her magic flower, and sweeter grew its breath, while the spirits lost still more power to tempt her. Meanwhile, green, flowering vines crept up the high dark wall, and hid its roughness from her sight, and over these she watched most tenderly, for soon, wherever green leaves and flowers bloomed, the wall beneath grew weak, and fell apart. Thus little Annie worked and hoped, till one by one the evil spirits flew away, and in their place came shining forms, with gentle eyes and smiling lips, who gathered round her with such loving words, and brought such strength and joy to Annie's heart that nothing evil dared to enter in ; while slowly sank the gloomy wall, and, over wreaths of fra grant flowers, she passed out into the pleasant world again, the fairy gift no longer pale and drooping, but now shining like a star upon her breast.

Then the low voice spoke again in Annie's ear, saying, "The dark, unlovely passions you have looked upon are in your heart; watch well while they are few and weak, lest they should darken your whole life, and shut out love and happiness forever. Remember well the lessons of the dream, dear child, and let the shining spirits make your heart their home."

And with that voice sounding in her ear, little Annie woke to find it was a dream; but like other dreams, it did not pass away; and as she sat alone, bathed in the rosy morning light, and watched the forest waken into life, she thought of the strange forms she had seen, and, looking down upon the flower on her breast, she silently resolved to strive, as she had striven in her dream, to bring back light and beauty to its faded leaves, by being what the Fairy hoped to render her, a patient, gentle little child. And as the thought came to her mind, the flower raised its drooping head, and, looking up into the earnest little face bent over it, seemed by its fragrant breath to answer Annie's silent thought, and strengthened her for what might come.

Meanwhile the forest was astir, birds sang their gay good-morrows from tree to tree, while leaf and flower turned to greet the sun, who rose up smiling on the world ; and so beneath the forest boughs and through the dewy fields went little Annie home, better and wiser for her dream.

Autumn flowers were dead and gone, yellow leaves lay rustling on the ground, bleak winds went whistling through the naked trees, and cold, white winter snow fell softly down ; yet now, when all without looked dark and dreary, on little Annie's breast the fairy flower bloomed more beautiful than ever.   The memory of her dream had never passed away, and through trial and temptation she had been true, and kept her resolution still unbroken ; seldom now did the warning bell sound in her ear, and seldom did the flower's fragrance cease to float about her, or the fairy light to brighten all whereon it fell.

So, through the long, cold Winter, Little Annie
dwelt like a sunbeam in her home, each day growing richer in the love of others, and happier in
herself; often was she tempted, but, remembering
her dream, she listened only to the music of the
fairy bell, and the unkind thought or feeling fled
away, the smiling spirits of gentleness and love
nestled in her heart, and all was bright again.

So better and happier grew the child, fairer
and sweeter grew the flower, till Spring came
smiling over the earth, and woke the flowers, set
free the streams, and welcomed back the birds;
then daily did the happy child sit among her
flowers, longing for the gentle Elf to come again,
that she might tell her gratitude for all the
magic gift had done.

At length one day, as she sat singing in the
sunny nook where all her fairest flowers bloomed,
weary with gazing at the far-off sky for the little
form she hoped would come, she bent to look
with joyful love upon her bosom flower; and as
she looked, its folded leaves spread wide apart,
and, rising slowly from the deep white cup, ap-

LITTLE ANNIE AND THE FAIRY.

peared the smiling face of the lovely Elf whose
coming she had waited for so long.

"Dear Annie, look for me no longer; I am
here on your breast, for you have learned to love
my gift, and it has done its work most faithfully
and well," the Fairy said, as she looked into the
happy child's bright face, and laid her little arms
most tenderly about her neck.

"And now have I brought another gift from
Fairy Land, as a fit reward for you, dear child,"
she said, when Annie had told her gratitude and
love; then, touching the child with her shining
wand, the Fairy bid her look and listen silently.

And suddenly the world seemed changed to
Annie; for the air was filled with strange, sweet
sounds, and all around her floated lovely forms.
In every flower sat little smiling Elves, singing
gayly as they rocked amid the leaves. On every
breeze, bright, airy spirits came floating by; some
fanned her cheek with their cool breath, and
waved her long hair to and fro, while others rang
the flower-bells, and made a pleasant rustling
among the leaves. In the fountain, where the
w.ter danced and sparkled in the sun, astride of

every drop she saw merry little spirits, who plashed and floated in the clear, cool waves, and sang as gayly as the flowers, on whom they scattered glittering dew. The tall trees, as their branches rustled in the wind, sang a low, dreamy song, while the waving grass was filled with little voices she had never heard before. Butterflies whispered lovely tales in her ear, and birds sang cheerful songs in a sweet language she had never understood before. Earth and air seemed filled with beauty and with music she had never dreamed of until now.

"O tell us what it means, dear Fairy! is it another and lovelier dream, or is the earth in truth so beautiful as this?" she cried, looking with wondering joy upon the Elf, who lay upon the flower in her breast.

"Yes, it is true, dear child," replied the Fairy, "and few are the mortals to whom we give this lovely gift; what to you is now so full of music and light, to others is but a pleasant summer world; they never know the language of butterflies or bird or flower, and they are blind to all that I have given you the power to see. These

Flower Fables—12

fair things are your friends and playmates now,
and they will teach you many pleasant lessons,
and give you many happy hours; while the
garden where you once sat, weeping sad and
bitter tears, is now brightened by your own happiness, filled with loving friends by your own
kindly thoughts and feelings; and thus rendered
a pleasant summer home for the gentle, happy
child, whose bosom flower will never fade. And
now, dear Annie, I must go; but every Spring-
time, with the earliest flowers, will I come again
to visit you, and bring some fairy gift. Guard
well the magic flower, that I may find all fair and
bright when next I come."

Then, with a kind farewell, the gentle Fairy
floated upward through the sunny air, smiling
down upon the child, until she vanished in the
soft, white clouds, and little Annie stood alone in
her enchanted garden, where all was brightened
with the radiant light, and fragrant with the perfume of her fairy flower.

When Moonlight ceased, Summer-Wind laid
down her rose-leaf fan, and, leaning back in her
acorn cup, told this tale of———

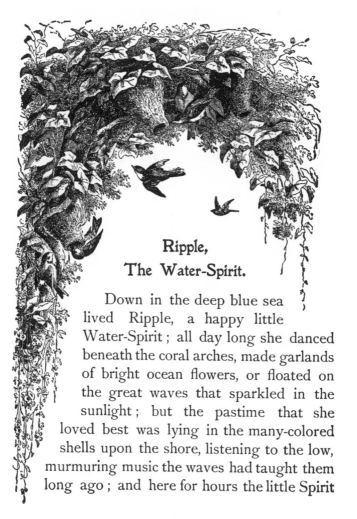

Ripple,
The Water-Spirit.

Down in the deep blue sea
lived Ripple, a happy little
Water-Spirit; all day long she danced
beneath the coral arches, made garlands
of bright ocean flowers, or floated on
the great waves that sparkled in the
sunlight; but the pastime that she
loved best was lying in the many-colored
shells upon the shore, listening to the low,
murmuring music the waves had taught them
long ago; and here for hours the little Spirit

RIPPLE STARTS ON HER MISSION.

lay watching the sea and sky, while singing gayly
to herself.

But when tempests rose, she hastened down
below the stormy billows, to where all was calm
and still, and with her sister Spirits waited till
it should be fair again, listening sadly, meanwhile, to the cries of those whom the wild waves
wrecked and cast into the angry sea, and who
soon came floating down, pale and cold, to the
Spirits' pleasant home; then they wept pitying
tears above the lifeless forms, and laid them in
quiet graves, where flowers bloomed, and jewels
sparkled in the sand.

This was Ripple's only grief, and she often
thought of those who sorrowed for the friends
they loved, who now slept far down in the dim
and silent coral caves, and gladly would she have
saved the lives of those who lay around her; but
the great ocean was far mightier than all the tender-hearted Spirits dwelling in its bosom. Thus
she could only weep for them, and lay them down
to sleep where no cruel waves could harm them
more.

One day, when a fearful storm raged far and

wide, and the Spirits saw great billows rolling like
heavy clouds above their heads, and heard the
wild winds sounding far away, down through the
foaming waves a little child came floating to their
home; its eyes were closed as if in sleep, the
long hair fell like seed-weed round its pale, cold
face, and the little hands still clasped the shells
they had been gathering on the beach, when the
great waves swept it into the troubled sea.

With tender tears the Spirits laid the little
form to rest upon its bed of flowers, and, singing
mournful songs, as if to make its sleep more calm
and deep, watched long and lovingly above it, till
the storm had died away, and all was still again.

While Ripple sang above the little child,
through the distant roar of winds and waves
she heard a wild, sorrowing voice, that seemed to
call for help. Long she listened, thinking it was
but the echo of their own plaintive song, but high
above the music still sounded the sad, wailing cry.
Then, stealing silently away, she glided up
through the foam and spray, till, through the
parting clouds, the sun shone upon her from
the tranquil sky, and, guided by the mournful

sound, she floated on, till, close before her on the
beach, she saw a woman stretching forth her arms,
and with a sad, imploring voice praying the rest-
less sea to give her back the little child it had so
cruelly borne away. But the waves dashed foaming up among the bare rocks at her feet, mingling their cold spray with her tears, and gave no
answer to her prayer.

When Ripple saw the mother's grief, she
longed to comfort her; so, bending tenderly
beside her, where she knelt upon the shore, the
little Spirit told her how her child lay softly sleeping, far down in a lovely place, where sorrowing
tears were shed, and gentle hands lay garlands
over him. But all in vain she whispered kindly
words; the weeping mother only cried:

"Dear Spirit, can you use no charm or spell
to make the waves bring back my child, as full of
life and strength as when they swept him from
my side? O give me back my little child, or let
me lie beside him in the bosom of the cruel sea."

"Most gladly will I help you if I can, though I
have little power to use; then grieve no more, for
I will search both earth and sea, to find some

friend who can bring back all you have lost.
Watch daily on the shore, and if I do not come
again, then you will know that my search has
been in vain. Farewell, poor mother, you shall
see your little child again, if Fairy power can win
him back." And with these words Ripple sprang
into the sea; while smiling through her tears, the
woman watched the gentle Spirit, till her bright
crown vanished in the waves.

When Ripple reached her home, she hastened
to the palace of the Queen, and told her of the
little child, the sorrowing mother, and the promise
she had made.

"Good little Ripple," said the Queen, when
she had told her all, "your promise never can be
kept; there is no power below the sea to work
this charm, and you can never reach the Fire-
Spirits' home, to win from them a flame to warm
the little body into life. I pity the poor mother,
and I would most gladly help her; but alas! I
am a Spirit like yourself, and cannot serve you
as I long to do."

"Ah, dear Queen! if you had seen her sorrow,
you too would seek to keep the promise I have

made. I cannot let her watch for me in vain, till I have done my best: then tell me where the Fire-Spirits dwell, and I will ask of them the flame that shall give life to the little child and such happiness to the sad, lonely mother: show me the path and let me go."

"It is far, far away, high up above the sun, where no Spirit ever dared to venture yet," replied the Queen. "I cannot show the path, for it is through the air. Dear Ripple, do not go, for you can never reach that distant place: some harm most surely will befall; and then how shall we live, without our dearest, gentlest Spirit? Stay here with us in your own pleasant home, and think no more of this, for I can not let you go."

But Ripple would not break the promise she had made, and besought so earnestly, and with such pleasing words, that the Queen at last with sorrow gave consent, and Ripple joyfully prepared to go. She, with her sister Spirits, built up a tomb of delicate, bright-colored shells, wherein the child might lie, till she should come to wake him into life; then, praying them to watch most faithfully above it, she said farewell, and floated bravely forth, on her unknown journey, far away.

"I will search the broad earth till I find a path up to the sun, or some kind friend who will carry me; for, alas! I have no wings, and cannot glide through the blue air as through the sea," said Ripple to herself, as she went dancing over the waves, which bore her swiftly onward towards a distant shore.

Long she journeyed through the pathless ocean, with no friends to cheer her, save the white sea-birds who went sweeping by, and only stayed to dip their wise wings at her side, and then flew silently away. Sometimes great ships sailed by, and then with longing eyes did the little Spirit gaze up at the faces that looked down upon the sea; for often they were kind and pleasant ones, and she gladly would have called to them and ask them to be friends. But they would never understand the strange, sweet language that she spoke, or even see the lovely face that smiled at them above the waves; her blue, transparent garments were but water to their eyes, and the pearl chains in her hair but foam and sparkling spray; so, hoping that the sea would be most gentle with them, silently she floated on her way, and left them far behind.

At length green hills were seen, and the waves gladly bore the little Spirit on, till, rippling gently over soft white sand, they left her on the pleasant shore.

"Ah, what a lovely place it is?" said Ripple, as she passed through the sunny valleys, where flowers began to bloom, and young leaves rustled on the trees.

"Why are you all so gay, dear birds?" she asked, as their cheerful voices sounded far and near; "is there a festival over the earth, that all is so beautiful and bright?"

"Do you know that Spring is coming? the warm winds whispered it days ago, and we are learning the sweetest songs, to welcome her, when she shall come," sang the lark, soaring away as the music gushed from his little throat.

"And shall I see her, Violet, as she journeys over the earth?" asked Ripple again.

"Yes, you will meet her soon, for the sunlight told me she was near; tell her we long to see her again, and are waiting to welcome her back," said the blue flower, dancing for joy on her stem, as she nodded and smiled on the Spirit.

"I will ask Spring where the Fire-Spirits dwell; she travels over the earth each year, and surely can show me the way," thought Ripple, as she went journeying on.

Soon she saw Spring come smiling over the earth; sunbeams and breezes floated before, and then, with her white garments covered with flowers, with wreaths in her hair, and dew-drops and seeds falling fast from her hands, the beautiful season came singing by.

"Dear Spring, will you listen, and help a poor little Spirit, who seeks far and wide for the Fire-Spirits' home?" cried little Ripple; and then told why she was there, and begged her to tell what she sought.

"The Fire-Spirits' home is far, far away, and I cannot guide you there; but Summer is coming behind me," said Spring, "and she may know better than I. But I will give you a breeze to help you on your way; it will never tire or fail, but bear you easily over land and sea. Farewell, little Spirit! I would gladly do more, but voices are calling me far and wide, and I cannot stay."

"Many thanks, kind Spring!" cried Ripple, as she floated away on the breeze; "give a kindly word to the mother who waits on the shore, and tell her I have not forgotten my vow, but hope soon to see her again."

Then Spring flew on with her sunshine and flowers, and Ripple went swiftly over hill and vale, till she came to the land where Summer was dwelling. Here the sun shone down on early fruit, the winds blew freshly over fields of fragrant hay, and rustled with pleasant sound among the green leaves in the forests; heavy dews fell softly down at night, and long, bright days brought strength and beauty to the blossoming earth.

"Now I must seek for Summer," said Ripple, as she sailed slowly through the sunny sky.

"I am here, what would you with me, little Spirit?" said a musical voice in her ear; and, floating by her side, she saw a graceful form, with green robes fluttering in the air, whose pleasant face looked kindly on her, from beneath a crown of golden sunbeams that cast a warm, bright glow on all beneath.

Then Ripple told her tale, and asked where she should go ; but Summer answered :

"I can tell no more than my young sister Spring where you may find the Spirits that you seek ; but I too, like her, will give you a gift to aid you. Take this sunbeam from my crown ; it will cheer and brighten the most gloomy path through which you may pass. Farewell! I shall carry tidings of you to the watcher by the sea, if in my journey round the world I find her there."

And Summer, giving her the sunbeam, passed away over the distant hills, leaving all green and bright behind her.

So Ripple journeyed on again, till the earth below her shone with yellow harvests waving in the sun, and the air was filled with cheerful voices, as the reapers sang among the fields or in the pleasant vineyards, where purple fruit hung gleaming through the leaves ; while the sky above was cloudless, and the changing forest-trees shone like a many-colored garland, over hill and plain ; and here, along the ripening corn-fields, with bright wreaths of crimson leaves and golden wheat-ears in her hair and on her purple mantle,

stately Autumn passed, with a happy smile on her
calm face, as she went scattering generous gifts
from her full arms.

But when the wandering Spirit came to her,
and asked for what she sought, this season, like
the others, could not tell her where to go; so,
giving her a yellow leaf, Autumn said, as she
passed on,

"Ask Winter, little Ripple, when you come to
his cold home; he knows the Fire-Spirits well, for
when he comes they fly to the earth, to warm and
comfort those dwelling there; and perhaps he can
tell you where they are. So take this gift of
mine, and when you meet his chilly winds, fold it
about you, and sit warm beneath its shelter, till
you come to sunlight again. I will carry comfort
to the patient woman, as my sisters have already
done, and tell her you are faithful still."

Then went on the never-tiring Breeze, over
forest, hill, and field, till the sky drew dark, and
bleak winds whistled by. Then Ripple, folded in
the soft, warm leaf, looked sadly down on the
earth, that seemed to lie so desolate and still beneath its shroud of snow, and thought how bitter

cold the leaves and flowers must be; for the little
Water-Spirit did not know that Winter spread a
soft white covering above their beds that they
might safely sleep below till Spring should waken
them again. So she went sorrowfully on, till
Winter, riding on a strong North-Wind, came
rushing by, with a sparkling ice-crown in his
streaming hair, while from beneath his crimson
cloak, where glittering frost-work shone like
silver threads, he scattered snow-flakes far and
wide.

"What do you seek with me, fair little Spirit,
that you come so bravely here amid my ice and
snow? Do not fear me; I am warm at heart,
though rude and cold without," said Winter,
looking kindly on her, while a bright smile shone
like sunlight on his pleasant face, as it glowed
and glistened in the frosty air.

When Ripple told him why she had come, he
pointed upward, where the sunlight dimly shone
through the heavy clouds, saying,

"Far off there, beside the sun, is the Fire-
Spirits' home; and the only path is up through
cloud and mist. It is a long, strange path for a

lonely little Spirit to be going ; the Fairies are wild,
wilful things, and in their play may harm and
trouble you. Come back with me, and do not go
this dangerous journey to the sky. I'll gladly
bear you home again, if you will come."

But Ripple said, "I cannot turn back now,
when I am nearly there. The Spirits surely will
not harm me, when I tell them why I am come ;
and if I win the flame, I shall be the happiest
Spirit in the sea, for my promise will be kept, and
the poor mother happy once again. So farewell,
Winter ! Speak to her gently, and tell her to
hope still, for I shall surely come."

"Adieu, little Ripple ! May good angels
watch above you ! journey bravely on, and take
this snow-flake that will never melt, as my gift,"
Winter cried, as the North-Wind bore him on,
leaving a cloud of falling snow behind.

" Now, dear Breeze," said Ripple, "fly straight
upward through the air, until we reach the place
we have long been seeking ; Sunbeam shall go
before to light the way, Yellow-leaf shall shelter
me from heat and rain, while Snow-flake shall lie
here beside me till it comes of use. So farewell

Flower Fables—13

to the pleasant earth, until we come again.   And now away, up to the sun !"

When Ripple first began her airy journey, all was dark and dreary; heavy clouds lay piled like hills around her, and a cold mist filled the air; but the Sunbeam, like a star, lit up the way, the leaf lay warmly round her, and the tireless wind went swiftly on.   Higher and higher they floated up, still darker and darker grew the air, closer the damp mist gathered, while the black clouds rolled and tossed, like great waves, to and fro.

"Ah!" sighed the weary little Spirit, "shall I never see the light again, or feel the warm winds on my cheek?   It is a dreary way indeed, and but for the Season's gifts I should have perished long ago; but the heavy clouds must pass away at last, and all be fair again.   So hasten on, good Breeze, and bring me quickly to my journey's end."

Soon the cold vapors vanished from her path, and sunshine shone upon her pleasantly; so she went gayly on, till she came among the stars, where many new, strange sights were to be seen. With wondering eyes she looked upon the bright

worlds that once seemed dim and distant, when
she gazed upon them from the sea ; but now they
moved around her, some shining with a softly
radiant light, some circled with bright, many-colored rings, while others burned with a red, angry
glare. Ripple would have gladly stayed to watch
them longer, for she fancied low, sweet voices
called her, and lovely faces seemed to look upon
her as she passed ; but higher up still, nearer to
the sun, she saw a far-off light, that glittered like
a brilliant star, and seemed to cast a rosy glow
along the sky.

" The Fire-Spirits surely must be there, and I
must stay no longer here," said Ripple. So
steadily she floated on, till straight before her lay
a broad, bright path, that led up to a golden arch,
beyond which she could see shapes flitting to and
fro. As she drew near, brighter glowed the sky,
hotter and hotter grew the air, till Ripple's leaf-
cloak shrivelled up, and could no longer shield
her from the heat ; then she unfolded the white
snow-flake, and, gladly wrapping the soft, cool
mantle round her, entered through the shining
arch.

Through the red mist that floated all around
her, she could see high walls of changing light,
where orange, blue, and violet flames went
flickering to and fro, making graceful figures as
they danced and glowed ; and underneath these
rainbow arches, little Spirits glided, far and near,
wearing crowns of fire, beneath which flashed
their wild, bright eyes, and as they spoke, sparks
dropped quickly from their lips, and Ripple saw
with wonder, through their garments of transparent light, that in each Fairy's breast there
burned a steady flame, that never wavered or
went out.

As thus she stood, the Spirits gathered round
her, and their hot breath would have scorched
her, but she drew the snow-cloak closer round
her, saying,

"Take me to your Queen, that I may tell her
why I am here, and ask for what I seek."

So through the long walls of many-colored fire,
they led her to a Spirit fairer than the rest, whose
crown of flames waved to and fro like golden
plumes, while, underneath her violet robe, the
light within her breast glowed bright and strong.

"This is our Queen," the Spirits said, bending low before her, as she turned her gleaming eyes upon the stranger they had brought.

Then Ripple told how she wandered round the world in search of them, how the Seasons had most kindly helped her on, by giving Sunbeam, Breeze, Leaf, and Flake, and how through many dangers, she had come at last to ask of them the magic flame that could give life to the little child again.

When she had told her tale, the Spirits whispered earnestly among themselves, while sparks fell thick and fast with every word ; at length the Fire-Queen said aloud,

"We cannot give you the flame you ask, for each of us must take a part of it from our own breasts, and this we will not do, for the brighter our bosom-fire burns, the lovelier we are. So do not ask us for this thing ; but any other gift we will most gladly give, for we feel kindly towards you, and will serve you in any way."

But Ripple asked no other boon, and weeping sadly, begged them not to send her back without the gift she had come so far to gain.

"O dear warm-hearted Spirts! give me each a little light from your own breasts, and surely they will glow brighter for this kindly deed; and I will thankfully repay it if I can." As thus she spoke, the Queen, who had spied out a chain of jewels Ripple wore upon her neck, replied:

"If you will give me those bright, sparkling stones, I will bestow on you a part of my own flame; for we have no such lovely things to wear about our necks, and I desire much to have them. Will you give it to me for what I offer, little Spirit?"

Joyfully Ripple gave her the chain; but, as soon as it touched her hand, the jewels melted like snow, and fell in bright drops to the ground; at this the Queen's eyes flashed, and the Spirits gathered angrily about poor Ripple, who looked sadly at the broken chain, and thought in vain what she could give, to win the thing she longed so earnestly for.

"I have many fairer gems than these, in my home below the sea; and I will bring all I can gather far and wide, if you will grant my prayer, and give me what I seek," she said, turning gently to the fiery Spirits, who were hovering fiercely around her.

"You must bring us each a jewel that will never vanish from our hands as these have done," they said, "and we will each give of our fire ; and when the child is brought to life, you must bring hither all the jewels you can gather from the depths of the sea, that we may try them here among the flames ; but if they melt away like these, then we shall keep you prisoner, till you give us back the light we lend. If you consent to this, then take our gift, and journey home again ; but fail not to return, or we shall seek you out."

And Ripple said she would consent, though she knew not if the jewels could be found ; still, thinking of the promise she had made, she forgot all else, and told the Spirits what they asked most surely should be done. So each one gave a little of the fire from their breasts, and placed the flame in a crystal vase, through which it glittered like a star.

Then bidding her remember all she had promised them, they led her to the golden arch, and said farewell.

So, down along the shining path, through mist
and cloud, she travelled back; till, far below, she
saw the broad blue sea she left so long ago.

Gladly she plunged into the clear, cool waves,
and floated back to her pleasant home, where the
Spirits gathered joyfully about her, listening with
tears and smiles, as she told all her many wanderings, and showed the crystal vase that she had
brought.

"Now come," said they, "and finish the good
work you have so bravely carried on."   So to the
quiet tomb they went, where, like a marble image,
cold and still, the little child was lying.   Then
Ripple placed the flame upon his breast, and
watched it gleam and sparkle there, while light
came slowly back into the once dim eyes, a rosy
glow shone over the pale face, and breath stole
through the parted lips; still brighter and
warmer burned the magic fire, until the child
awoke from his long sleep, and looked in smiling
wonder at the faces bending over him.

Then Ripple sang for joy, and, with her sister
Spirits, robed the child in graceful garments,
woven of bright sea-weed, while in his shining

hair they wreathed long garlands of their fairest flowers, and on his little arms hung chains of brilliant shells.

"Now come with us, dear child," said Ripple; "we will bear you safely up into the sunlight and pleasant air; for this is not your home, and yonder, on the shore, there waits a loving friend for you."

So up they went, through foam and spray, till on the beach, where the fresh winds played among her falling hair, and the waves broke sparkling at her feet, the lonely mother still stood gazing wistfully across the sea. Suddenly, upon a great blue billow that came rolling in, she saw the Water-Spirits smiling on her; and high aloft, in their white gleaming arms, her child stretched forth his hands to welcome her; while the little voice she so longed to hear again cried gayly,

"See, dear mother, I am come; and look what lovely things the gentle Spirits gave, that I might seem more beautiful to you."

Then gently the great wave broke, and rolled back to the sea, leaving Ripple on the shore, and the child clasped in his mother's arms.

"O faithful little Spirit! I would gladly give some precious gift to show my gratitude for this kind deed, but I have nothing save this chain of little pearls ; they are the tears I shed, and the sea has changed them thus, that I might offer them to you," the happy mother said, when her first joy was passed, and Ripple turned to go.

"Yes, I will gladly wear your gift, and look upon it as my fairest ornament," the Water-Spirit said, and with the pearls upon her breast she left the shore, where the child was playing gayly to and fro, and the mother's glad smile shone upon her, till she sank beneath the waves.

And now another task was to be done ; her promise to the Fire-Spirits must be kept. So far and wide she searched among the caverns of the sea, and gathered all the brightest jewels shining there, and then upon her faithful Breeze once more went journeying through the sky.

The Spirits gladly welcomed her, and led her to the Queen, before whom she poured out the sparkling gems she had gathered with such toil and care, but when the Spirits tried to form them into crowns, they trickled from their hands like

colored drops of dew, and Ripple saw with fear
and sorrow how they melted one by one away,
till none of all the many she had brought re-
mained. Then the Fire-Spirits looked upon her
angrily, and when she begged them to be merciful,
and let her try once more saying,

"Do not keep me prisoner here. I cannot
breathe the flames that give you life, and but for
this snow-mantle I too should melt away, and
vanish like the jewels in your hands. O dear
Spirits, give me some other task, but let me go
from this warm place, where all is strange and
fearful to a Spirit of the sea."

They would not listen, and drew nearer, saying, while bright sparks showered from their lips.
"We will not let you go, for you have promised
to be ours if the gems you brought proved worthless; so fling away this cold white cloak, and
bathe with us in the fire fountains, and help us
bring back to our bosom flames and light we gave
you for the child."

Then Ripple sank down on the burning floor,
and felt that her life was nearly done; for she
well knew the hot air of the fire-palace would be

death to her. The Spirits gathered round, and
began to lift her mantle off; but underneath they
saw the pearl chain, shining with a clear, soft
light, that only glowed more brightly when they
laid their hands upon it.

"O give us this!" cried they; "it is far lovelier than all the rest, and does not melt away like
them; and see how brilliantly it glitters in our
hands. If we may have but this, all will be well,
and you are once more free."

And Ripple, safe again beneath her snow-flake,
gladly gave the chain to them; and told them how
the pearls they now placed proudly on their
breasts were formed of tears, which but for them
might still be flowing. Then the Spirits smiled
most kindly on her, and would have put their
arms about her, and have kissed her cheek, but
she drew back, telling them that every touch of
theirs was like a wound to her.

"Then, if we may not tell our pleasure so, we
will show it in a different way, and give you a
pleasant journey home. Come out with us," the
Spirits said, "and see the bright path we have
made for you." So they led her to a lofty gate

and here, from sky to earth, a lovely rainbow arched its radiant colors in the sun.

"This is indeed a pleasant road," said Ripple. "Thank you, friendly Spirits, for your care; and now farewell. I would gladly stay yet longer, but we cannot dwell together, and I am longing sadly for my own cool home. Now Sunbeam, Breeze, Leaf, and Flake, fly back to the Seasons whence you came, and tell them that, thanks to their kind gifts, Ripple's work at last is done."

Then down along the shining pathway spread before her, the happy little Spirit glided to the sea. "Thanks, dear Summer-Wind," said the Queen; "we will remember the lessons you have each taught us, and when next we meet in Fern Dale, you shall tell us more. And now, dear Trip, call them from the lake, for the moon is sinking fast, and we must hasten home."

The Elves gathered about their Queen, and while the rustling leaves were still, and the flowers' sweet voices mingling with their own, they sang this

Fairy Song.

The moonlight fades from flower and
    tree,
   And the stars dim one by one;
The tale is told, the song is sung,
   And the Fairy feast is done.
The night-wind rocks the sleeping
    flowers,
   And sings to them, soft and low.
The early birds erelong will wake:
   'Tis time for the Elves to go.

O'er the sleeping earth we silently pass,
   Unseen by mortal eye,

And send sweet dreams, as we lightly **float**
 Through the quiet moonlit sky;
For the stars' soft eyes alone may **see**,
 And the flowers alone may know,
The feast we hold, the tales we **tell**:
 So't is time for the Elves to go.

From bird, and blossom, and be**e**,
 We learn the lesson they teach;
And seek, by kindly deeds, to wi**n**
 A loving friend in each.
And though unseen on earth we dw**ell**,
 Sweet voices whisper low,
And gentle hearts most joyously gr**eet**
 The Elves where'er they go.

When next **we** meet in the Fairy de**ll**,
 May the silver moon's soft light
Shine then on faces gay as n**ow**,
 And Elfin hearts as light.

Now spread each wing, for the eastern sky
With sunlight soon will glow.
The morning star will light us home :
Farewell! for the Elves must go.

As the music ceased, with soft, rustling sound
the Elves spread their shining wings, and flew
silently over the sleeping earth; the flowers
closed their bright eyes, the little winds were
still, for the feast was over, and the Fairy lessons
ended.

THE END.